S∧P
education

Singapore
MATH
CHALLENGE

Terry Chew B.Sc.

GRADE
4+

P9-EAX-949

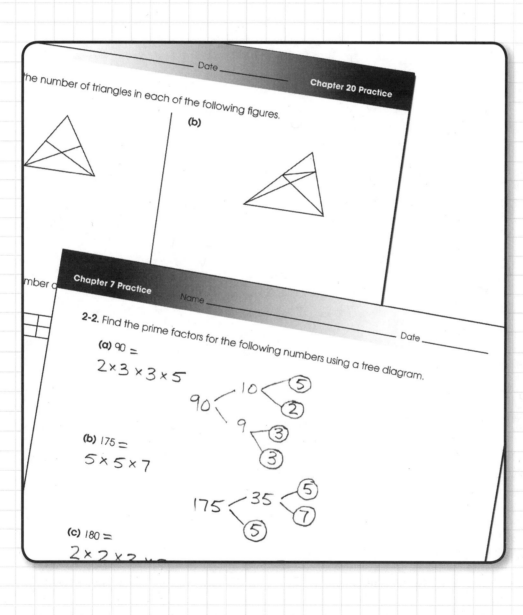

Date _____

Chapter 20 Practice

the number of triangles in each of the following figures.

(b)

mber o

Chapter 7 Practice

Name _____

2-2. Find the prime factors for the following numbers using a tree diagram.

Date _____

(a) 90 =

2 × 3 × 3 × 5

(b) 175 =

5 × 5 × 7

(c) 180 =

2 × 2 × 2

Thinking Kids®
An imprint of Carson-Dellosa Publishing LLC
Greensboro, NC

© Singapore Asia Publishers Pte Ltd

978-1-62399-074-9
Singapore Math Challenge

In *Singapore Math Challenge*, your child will find a variety of intriguing problems and problem-solving methods. Using the step-by-step techniques will help your son or daughter develop skill and creativity as a mathematical thinker.

What is Singapore Math?

Singapore's math curriculum has been recognized worldwide for its excellence in producing students highly skilled in mathematics. Students in Singapore regularly rank at the top of the world in mathematics on the Trends in International Mathematics and Science Study (TIMSS).

The Singapore Math curriculum aims to help students develop necessary concepts and skills for everyday life and to provide students with the ability to formulate, apply, and solve problems. The Singapore Primary (Elementary) Mathematics curriculum covers fewer topics, but in greater depth. Key concepts are introduced and built-on to reinforce mathematical ideas and thinking. Skills are typically taught a full year ahead of when similar skills are taught in the United States.

Singapore Math and the Common Core State Standards

Common Core State Standards in mathematics have been adopted by most U.S. states. These standards are designed to help prepare American students for success in college and in the global twenty-first century workforce. They outline clear, consistent, and rigorous expectations for learning in math.

In developing the Common Core State Standards, experts looked at educationally high-performing nations such as Singapore to identify the best approaches to learning. Singapore math standards are frequently cited in the research used to support the Common Core standards.

Common Core State Standards have raised the bar for American students. Strategies taught in *Singapore Math Challenge* will help students meet these new expectations.

Using *Singapore Math Challenge* Books

Each chapter focuses on a challenging, age-appropriate topic and demonstrates several clever problem-solving methods. Topics in this series include:

- **Basic Concepts:**
  New ways to understand counting, telling time, odd and even numbers, place value, fractions, averaging, and prime numbers

- **Operations:**
  Tricks for solving addition, subtraction, multiplication, and division problems

- **Strategies:**
  Creative and effective approaches to problem solving, including making lists and visual models, making assumptions, comparing and replacing, and working backward

- **Classic Problems:**
  Techniques for solving problems that have interested mathematicians through the ages, including intervals, numbers in a series, speed problems, age problems, and excess-and-shortage problems

- **Logic and IQ:**
  Brain-teasing patterns, puzzles, and logic problems to strengthen mathematical thinking

- **Applied and Advanced Topics:**
  Introductions to squares and cubes, perimeter, area, angles and triangles, percentages, and writing simple algebraic equations

Students should study the examples that begin each chapter and refer back to them often as they attempt to solve the problems. Blank space is provided for working each problem. A complete worked solution for each problem can be found in the back of the book.

Invite your student to think creatively and to try different methods when solving these challenging problems. Above all, encourage your child to approach math endeavors with confidence and to think of math as a fun and fascinating journey.

6

Chapter 1

Looking for a Pattern

In mathematics, there are various patterns: some are relatively straightforward and others are more challenging. We, therefore, have to think outside the box and be flexible in our search for answers.

Besides adding or subtracting the terms in a number pattern, applying multiplication, division or even the use of any two arithmetic skills may help in the solving of the problem.

In **Fibonacci numbers**, the third term in the number pattern is the sum of the first and second terms; the fourth term is the sum of the second and third terms; the fifth term is the sum of the third and fourth terms and so forth. In essence each term, after the first two terms, is the sum of two preceding terms.

978-1-62399-074-9
Singapore Math Challenge

Example: Complete each number pattern.

(a)   4,   7,   10,   13,   (   ),   ...

> **Analysis:** The difference between any two terms in the above number pattern is 3, so the next term must be $13 + 3 = 16$.

(b)   2,   6,   12,   20,   (   ),   ...

> **Analysis:** This is more interesting than the number pattern shown in (a). The second term is 4 more than the first one. Thereafter, the difference between any two terms increases by 2.

$$2 + ④ = 6$$
$$6 + 4 + ② = 12$$
$$12 + 4 + 2 + ② = 20$$

The next term is, therefore, $20 + 4 + 2 + 2 + 2 = 30$.

(c)   2,   6,   18,   (   ),   ...

> **Analysis:** In the above number pattern, it is difficult to make sense of the difference between any two numbers. The difference between the first and second terms is 4. The difference between the second and third terms is 12. Observe: the two differences will reveal that 12 is three times 4. So, the second term is three times the first term. The third term is three times the second term, and so on.

$$6 \div 2 = 3$$
$$18 \div 6 = 3$$
$$18 \times 3 = 54$$

The next term is 54.

(d)   44,   22,   20,   10,   8,   (   ),   (   )

Analysis: The above number pattern uses two arithmetic skills: division and subtraction. The first term is divided by 2 and the second term is subtracted by 2.

$$44 \div 2 = 22 \qquad\qquad 22 - 2 = 20$$
$$20 \div 2 = 10 \qquad\qquad 10 - 2 = 8$$
$$8 \div 2 = 4 \qquad\qquad 4 - 2 = 2$$

The next two terms are 4 and 2 respectively.

(e)   1,   1,   2,   3,   5,   8,   13,   (   ),   (   ),   55,   89,   ...

Analysis: This number pattern is an example of Fibonacci numbers.

$$13 + 8 = 21$$
$$21 + 13 = 34$$

The two terms are 21 and 34 respectively.

1. Complete each number pattern below.

(a) 1,   1,   2,   3,   5,   (   ),   (   ),   ...

(b) 1,   1,   1,   1,   4,   7,   13,   (   ),   ...

(c) 3,   5,   9,   15,   23,   33,   45,   (   ),   ...

(d) 1,   3,   6,   10,   (   ),   21,   28,   36,   ...

(e) 0,   3,   8,   15,   24,   (   ),   48,   63,   ...

(f) 1,   2,   6,   24,   120,   (   ),   5,040,   ...

(g) 0,   1,   3,   8,   21,   55,   (   ),   (   ),   ...

(h) 1,   3,   7,   15,   31,   (   ),   127,   ...

(i) 1,   1,   3,   7,   13,   (   ),   31,   ...

(j) 1,   2,   5,   13,   34,   89,   (   ),   (   ),   ...

2. *Ah, the magical trick of 9!*

Observe the pattern and write the correct answers in the brackets provided.

$$21 \times 9 = 189$$

$$321 \times 9 = 2,889$$

$$4,321 \times 9 = 38,889$$

$$54,321 \times 9 = (\qquad)$$

$$654,321 \times 9 = (\qquad)$$

$$7,654,321 \times 9 = (\qquad)$$

$$87,654,321 \times 9 = (\qquad)$$

$$987,654,321 \times 9 = (\qquad)$$

3. Complete the Pascal Triangle and write the correct answers in the brackets provided.

```
                    I
                I       I
            I       2       I
        I       3       3       I
    I       4       6       4       I
  I   (   )   (   )   (   )   (   )   I
 I  (   )  (   )  (   )  (   )  (   )  I
I  (   )  (   )  (   )  (   )  (   )  (   )  I
```

4. *The marvel of multiplication of 101!*

Observe the pattern and write the correct answers in the brackets provided.

$$101 \times 11 = 1,111$$

$$101 \times 22 = 2,222$$

$$101 \times 33 = 3,333$$

$$101 \times 44 = (\qquad)$$

$$101 \times 55 = (\qquad)$$

$$101 \times 66 = (\qquad)$$

$$101 \times 77 = (\qquad)$$

$$101 \times 88 = (\qquad)$$

$$101 \times 99 = (\qquad)$$

5. What are the missing numbers in the number patterns below?

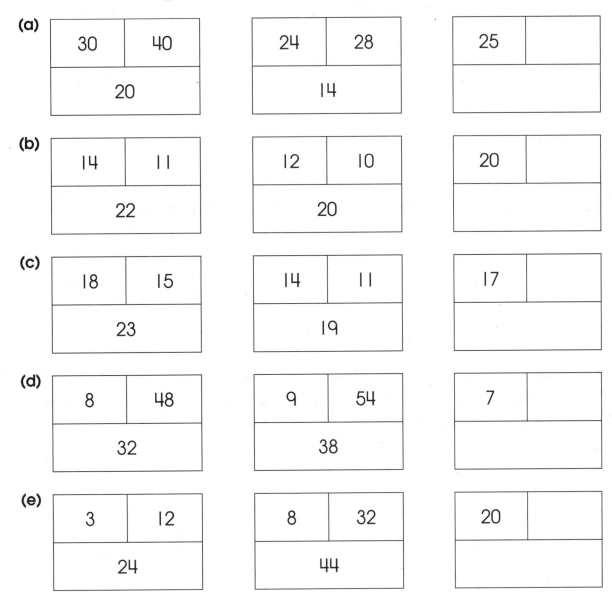

(a)

30	40
20	

24	28
14	

25	

(b)

14	11
22	

12	10
20	

20	

(c)

18	15
23	

14	11
19	

17	

(d)

8	48
32	

9	54
38	

7	

(e)

3	12
24	

8	32
44	

20	

978-1-62399-074-9
Singapore Math Challenge

6. Fill in each blank with digits from 1 to 9. Each digit may be used once only. The number on the left-hand side of the arrow is added to 12 to reach the number on the right-hand side.

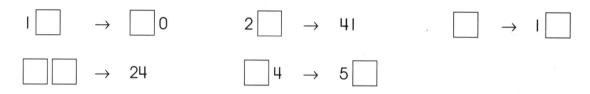

7. Fill in each blank with digits from 1 to 9. Each digit may be used once only. The number on the left-hand side of the arrow is multiplied by 4 before adding 5 to reach the number on the right-hand side.

8. Fill in each blank with digits from 1 to 9. Each digit may be used once only. The number on the left-hand side of the arrow is divided by 2 before subtracting 1 from it to reach the number on the right-hand side.

☐ → ☐   ☐☐ → ☐   30 → 1☐

4☐ → 22   ☐6 → 4☐

978-1-62399-074-9
Singapore Math Challenge

9. Fill in each blank with digits from 1 to 9. Each digit may be used once only. The number on the left-hand side of the arrow is multiplied by 2 before adding 3 to reach the number on the right-hand side.

1 ☐ → 3 ☐   1 ☐ → 31   ☐ 5 → ☐ 3

☐ 7 → 5 ☐   1 ☐ → 3 ☐

10. Can you put 32 balls in the boxes below so that there is an equal number of balls along each line?

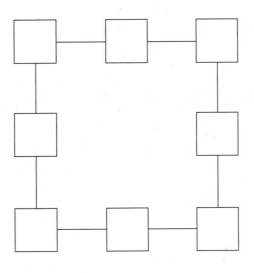

11. Find the eighth term of the sequence.

   3,   5,   9,   15,   23,   33,   45,   (   ),   ...

12. Find the eighth term of the sequence.

   1,   4,   11,   29,   76,   199,   521,   (   ),   ...

13. Find the sixth term of the sequence.

   1,   4,   9,   16,   25,   (   ),   49,   64,   ...

14. Find the seventh and eighth terms of the sequence.

   1,   2,   4,   7,   11,   16,   (   ),   (   ),   ...

15. Find the seventh and eighth terms of the sequence.

   2,   4,   8,   14,   22,   32,   (   ),   (   ),   ...

978-1-62399-074-9
Singapore Math Challenge

16. Find the sixth, seventh and eighth terms of the sequence.

3,   4,   9,   10,   15,   (   ),   (   ),   (   ),   ...

17. Find the seventh and eighth terms of the sequence.

1,   3,   6,   8,   16,   18,   (   ),   (   ),   76,   78,   ...

18. Which of the following sequences is different from the rest?

(a) 1,   1,   2,   3,   5,   8,   13,   ...

(b) 0,   2,   2,   4,   6,   10,   16,   ...

(c) 1,   3,   4,   7,   11,   18,   29,   ...

(d) 1,   2,   3,   6,   11,   20,   37,   ...

19. Find the missing number in each number pattern.

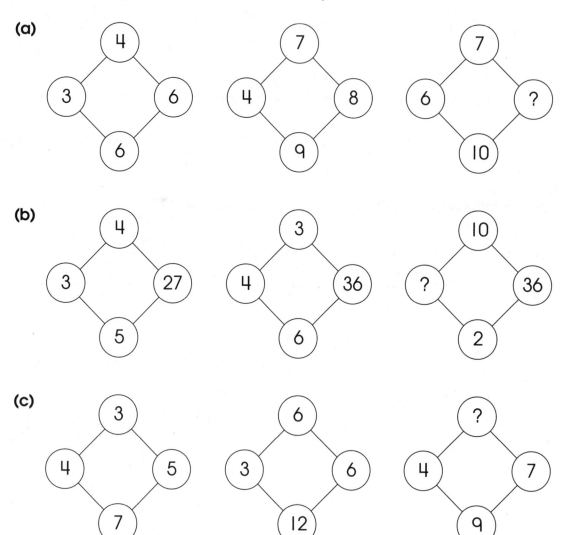

(a)

(b)

(c)

20. Felicia saved $10 in January. She saved $20 in February. The amount of money she saved in March was the total amount of money she had saved in January and February. The amount of money she saved in April was the total amount of money she had saved in February and March. If she saved in this pattern up to October,

(a) in which month did she save $210?

(b) how much did she save in October?

21. Write the missing numbers in the brackets provided.

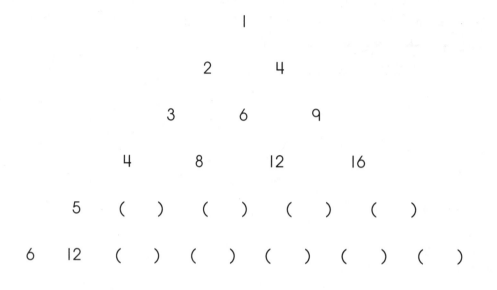

```
                            1

                     2            4

                  3       6            9

              4       8       12          16

          5   (   )   (   )   (   )   (   )

      6   12  (   )   (   )   (   )   (   )   (   )
```

The Story of Gauss

Carl Gauss, one of the greatest mathematicians, was born in 1777 in Brunswick, Germany. He was gifted in mathematics and showed a talent in that field at an early age.

A popular story about this mathematical genius goes like this.

One day, his elementary school teacher asked all the students to find the value of

$$1 + 2 + 3 + 4 + 5 + 6 + 7 + 8 + 9 + \cdots + 98 + 99 + 100$$

It was his teacher's hope to use the lengthy addition problem to quiet the class.

Surprisingly, the mathematical prodigy worked out the correct answer almost instantaneously!

Well? Don't you want to know how he did it?

Gauss added 1 to 100, 2 to 99, 3 to 98, ... Each pair added to 101. Since there were 50 such pairs from integers 1 to 100, he multiplied 101 by 50 to get the final answer, 5,050.

978-1-62399-074-9
Singapore Math Challenge

Example 1: Find the value of 1 + 2 + 3 + 4 + 5 + 6 + 7 + 8.

    Analysis: We can make 4 pairs of 9.

$$1 + 8 = 9$$
$$2 + 7 = 9$$
$$3 + 6 = 9$$
$$4 + 5 = 9$$

Instead of adding up all the numbers, we simply multiply 4 by 9 to get 36.

Example 2: Find the value of 1 + 2 + 3 + 4 + 5 + 6 + 7 + 8 + 9 + 10.

    Analysis: We can make 5 pairs of 11.

$$1 + 10 = 11$$
$$2 + 9 = 11$$
$$3 + 8 = 11$$
$$4 + 7 = 11$$
$$5 + 6 = 11$$

Instead of adding up all the numbers, we multiply 5 by 11 to get 55.

Example 3: Find the value of $1 + 2 + 3 + 4 + 5 + 6 + 7 + 8 + 9 + 10 + 11 + 12 + 13 + 14 + 15$.

Analysis: We can make 7 pairs of 16.

$$1 + 15 = 16$$
$$2 + 14 = 16$$
$$3 + 13 = 16$$
$$4 + 12 = 16$$
$$5 + 11 = 16$$
$$6 + 10 = 16$$
$$7 + 9 = 16$$

Now, what about the number that is not in pairs?

We just have to add the remaining number to the product of the pairs.

$$7 \times 16 = 112$$
$$112 + 8 = 120$$

In some situations where you need to find the remaining number, just take the sum of the first and last numbers in the sequence and divide by 2.

I. Find the value of 4 + 6 + 8 + 10 + 12 + 14.

2. Find the value of 2 + 3 + 4 + 5 + 6 + 7 + 8.

3. Find the value of 3 + 4 + 5 + 6 + 7 + 8 + 9 + 10.

4. Find the value of 5 + 6 + 7 + 8 + 9 + 10 + 11.

5. Find the value of 16 + 18 + 20 + 22 + 24 + 26 + 28 + 30.

6. Find the value of 3 + 5 + 7 + 9 + 11 + 13 + 15.

7. Find the value of 5 + 8 + 11 + 14 + 17 + 20.

8. Find the value of 9 + 13 + 17 + 21 + 25 + 29.

9. Find the value of $1 + 2 + 3 + 4 + \cdots + 47 + 48 + 49 + 50$.

10. Find the value of $2 + 4 + 6 + 8 + \cdots + 44 + 46 + 48 + 50$.

11. Find the value of $1 + 3 + 5 + 7 + \cdots + 43 + 45 + 47 + 49$.

12. Find the value of $1 + 2 + 3 + 4 + \cdots + 97 + 98 + 99 + 100$.

13. Cindy saved $15 in the first month, $30 in the second month, $45 in the third month, and so forth. The amount of money she saved in the last month was $120. How much money did Cindy save in all?

14. There are 12 rows of seats in a cinema. There are 10 seats in the first row, 12 seats in the second row, 14 seats in the third row, and so forth. How many seats are there in the cinema altogether?

15. Danny read 20 pages of a storybook on the first day. On the second day, the number of pages he read increased by 5. The number of pages he read on the third day was 10 more than that of the first day, the number of pages he read on the fourth day was 5 more than that of the third day, and so forth. If he read the remaining 80 pages of the storybook on the last day, how many pages were there in the storybook?

16. There are 16 rows of seats in a school auditorium. There are 75 seats in the last row. If there is an increase of 3 seats in each row, starting from the first row,

    (a) how many seats are there in the first row?

    (b) how many seats are there in the school auditorium?

17. Given a sequence 3, 3, 1, 9, 4, 3, 3, 1, 9, 4, 3, 3, 1, 9, 4, ...

    (a) What is the 33rd number?

    (b) What is the sum of the first 40 terms?

978-1-62399-074-9
Singapore Math Challenge

18. There were 7 books in a series of mystery novels. Each book was written and published every two years. The fifth book in this series was written and published in 2003. In which years were the remaining books written and published?

19. There are 54 tennis balls altogether. Are you able to group them into 10 groups so that each group has a different number of balls?

20. There are 20 players in a table tennis competition. Each player must play exactly one match against every other player. How many matches are there in the competition?

21. The grandfather clock chimes once when it is 1 o'clock, chimes twice when it is 2 o'clock, chimes three times when it is 3 o'clock and so forth.

(a) How many times will it chime between 12 noon and 11 o'clock at night?

(b) How many times will it chime in 24 hours?

Working Backward

Some problems are difficult to solve if we try to use standard methods. But if the problem is worked backward, it makes the problem-solving systematic and easy.

Three characteristics of this type of problem are:

(1) we start with something we do not know,

(2) the end answer is given to us,

(3) the problem will go through a series of operations.

Students are encouraged to do it systematically by writing or drawing the original operations stated in the problem. By reversing the operations while working backward, the answer will be obtained!

Example 1: Work backward by changing "+" to "−", "−" to "+", "×" to "÷" and finally "÷" to "×."

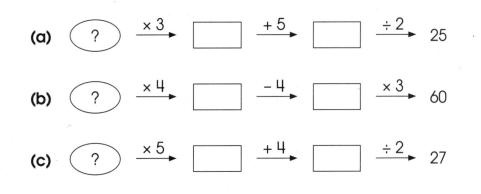

(a) ? ×3 → ▢ +5 → ▢ ÷2 → 25

(b) ? ×4 → ▢ −4 → ▢ ×3 → 60

(c) ? ×5 → ▢ +4 → ▢ ÷2 → 27

Solution:

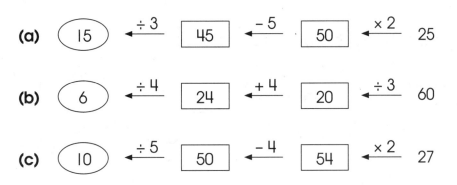

(a) 15 ←÷3 45 ←−5 50 ←×2 25

(b) 6 ←÷4 24 ←+4 20 ←÷3 60

(c) 10 ←÷5 50 ←−4 54 ←×2 27

978-1-62399-074-9
Singapore Math Challenge

Example 2: I am a tricky number. First, you add 5 to me, multiply the sum by 5, subtract 5 from the product and divide the difference by 5. The result will be 5. What am I?

Solution:

We write out the problem as shown below.

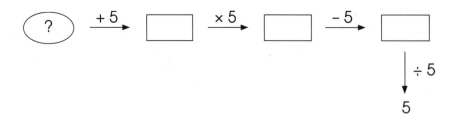

We work backward by changing the signs accordingly.

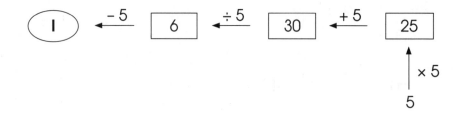

978-1-62399-074-9
Singapore Math Challenge

Example 3: There were 70 books on the first and second shelves of a bookcase. 28 books from the second shelf were sold. 15 books on the first shelf were moved to the second shelf. The two shelves then had the same number of books. How many books were there on each shelf at first?

Solution:

70 – 28 = 42

There were 42 books left.

42 ÷ 2 = 21

There were 21 books on each shelf in the end.

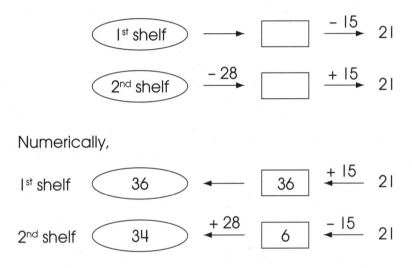

Numerically,

1st shelf (36) ← [36] ←+ 15← 21

2nd shelf (34) ←+ 28← [6] ←– 15← 21

There were 36 books on the first shelf and 34 books on the second shelf at first.

Example 4: Alan, Benny and Charles had a total of $750 at first. Alan gave $30 to Benny. Benny gave $50 to Charles. Each of them then had the same amount of money. How much money did each boy have at first?

Solution:

$750 ÷ 3 = $250

Each boy had $250 in the end.

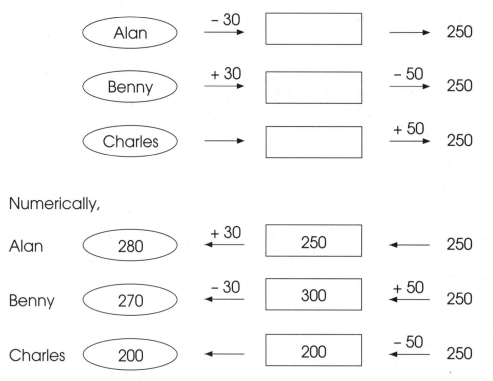

Numerically,

Alan had $280, Benny had $270 and Charles had $200 at first.

978-1-62399-074-9
Singapore Math Challenge

Example 5: Sabrina went up 5 floors to her grandmother's apartment to collect a prune cake. She went down 8 floors to pass the prune cake to her cousin. She then went up another 2 floors to look for a friend who lived on the 10th floor to do homework together. On what floor does Sabrina live?

Solution:

Sabrina

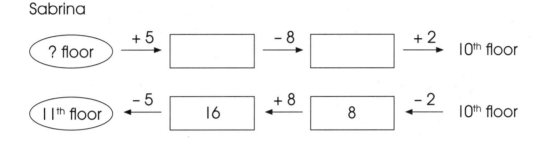

Sabrina lives on the 11th floor.

Example 6: During a shopping trip, Cindy spent half of her money in the first shop. She spent $2 more than half of her remaining money in the second shop. She was left with $30 in the end. How much money did Cindy have at first?

Solution:

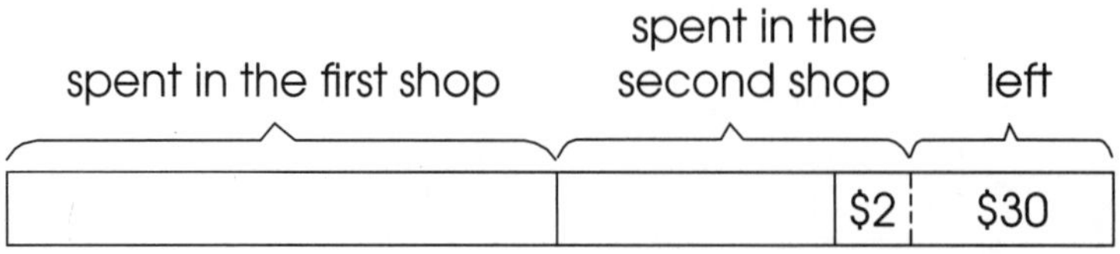

spent in the first shop   spent in the second shop   left

| | $2 | $30 |

From the above drawing,

$\frac{1}{4}$ of Cindy's money $\rightarrow$ $30 + $2 = $32

$32 × 4 = $128

Cindy had $128 at first.

I. Work backward by changing "+" to "−", "−" to "+", "×" to "÷" and finally "÷" to "×."

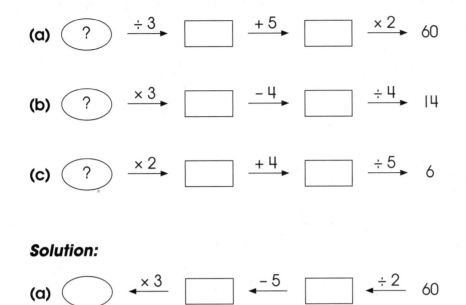

(a) (?) —÷ 3→ [   ] —+ 5→ [   ] —× 2→ 60

(b) (?) —× 3→ [   ] —− 4→ [   ] —÷ 4→ 14

(c) (?) —× 2→ [   ] —+ 4→ [   ] —÷ 5→ 6

Solution:

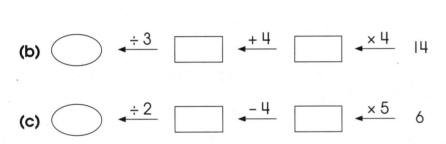

(a) ( ) ←× 3— [   ] ←− 5— [   ] ←÷ 2— 60

(b) ( ) ←÷ 3— [   ] ←+ 4— [   ] ←× 4— 14

(c) ( ) ←÷ 2— [   ] ←− 4— [   ] ←× 5— 6

2. A number is added to 6. The sum is then multiplied by 6. Then, 6 is again subtracted from the product. When the difference is divided by 6, the result is still 6. What is this number?

3. A number is added to 3. The sum is then multiplied by 5. When 8 is subtracted from the product, the result is 12. What is this number?

978-1-62399-074-9
Singapore Math Challenge

4. On Monday, half of the total number of books were loaned out. Another 87 books were loaned out the next day. There were only 43 books left in the library. How many books were there in the library at first?

5. A white rabbit managed to gather some mushrooms. It gave 6 mushrooms to its best friend, Brownie, before it gathered 10 more mushrooms. The white rabbit had 19 mushrooms left after another friend, Spot, borrowed 5 mushrooms. How many mushrooms did the white rabbit gather at first?

6. There were 36 cars in parking lot A and parking lot B altogether. 4 cars drove out from parking lot A. 5 cars drove out from parking lot B to parking lot A. The number of cars in parking lot A was 3 times those in parking lot B. How many cars were there in parking lot A and parking lot B at first?

7. 16 sparrows were resting on two trees. 2 sparrows flew away from the second tree, 5 sparrows flew from the first tree to the second tree. The two trees now had the same number of sparrows. How many sparrows were there on the first tree and how many sparrows were there on the second tree at first?

8. Cindy and Elaine had $60 altogether. If Cindy gave Elaine $12 and Elaine gave Cindy $10, Cindy would have three times as much money as Elaine. How much money did each of them have at first?

9. There were 90 marbles in two boxes. 15 marbles were transferred from Box A to Box B. 18 marbles from Box B were then transferred back to Box A. The number of marbles in Box A was twice the number of marbles in Box B. How many marbles were in each box at first?

10. 16 flying squirrels were resting on two branches of a tree. 2 flying squirrels from each branch were frightened by visitors and flew away. Another 6 flying squirrels flew from the first branch to the second branch. After 4 flying squirrels flew back to the first branch from the second branch, the number of flying squirrels on the first branch was twice the number of flying squirrels on the second branch. How many flying squirrels were on each branch at first?

978-1-62399-074-9
Singapore Math Challenge

11. A bus with some commuters left the bus terminal. At the first bus stop, 4 commuters boarded and 6 commuters got off. The number of commuters doubled after the second bus stop. At the third bus stop, 3 commuters got off and there were 15 commuters on the bus. How many commuters were on the bus when it left the bus terminal?

12. Debra went up 4 floors from her apartment to collect a birthday cake from her auntie. She walked down 3 floors to pass the cake to her friend. She then walked down another 3 floors to her uncle's house which was on the 6th floor. On which floor was Debra's apartment?

13. Cindy asked her grandfather about his age. Her grandfather replied, "You add 10 to my age, divide the sum by 4, subtract 15 from the quotient and multiply the difference by 10. You will get 100!" Can you help Cindy to find her grandfather's age?

14. A rope was cut in half. Half of the rope was cut in half again. After four such cuts, the length of one such rope was 1 m. What was the original length of the rope?

15. An egg-seller sold 2 eggs more than half the number of eggs in his basket. He then sold 2 eggs fewer than half of the remaining eggs in his basket. If he was left with 28 eggs, how many eggs were in the basket at first?

16. A minivan left a condominium with a number of passengers. 7 passengers got off and 10 passengers boarded the minivan at Evergreen Road. At Woodville Interchange, $\frac{1}{4}$ of the number of passengers got off and 12 passengers were left in the minivan. How many passengers were on the minivan when it left the condominium?

17. A basket of apples was given to the students in Class 3C and Class 3D. 3 more than half of the number of apples were given to the students in Class 3D. 2 more than the remaining half of the number of apples were given to Class 3C. There were 4 apples left in the basket. How many apples were there at first?

18. Alice used $4 to buy a comic. She used half of the remaining money to buy a magazine. Lastly, she used $1 more than half of the remaining money to buy a pen. She was left with $5. How much money had Alice at first?

19. Alex, Benny and Mike had $90 altogether. If Alex gave Benny $12, Benny gave Mike $13 and Mike gave Alex $5, the three boys had the same amount of money in the end. How much money did each boy have at first?

20. Alicia, Betty and Chloe have 90 books altogether. If Betty borrows 3 books from Alicia and lends 5 books to Chloe, the three girls have the same number of books in the end. How many books does each girl have at first?

978-1-62399-074-9
Singapore Math Challenge

The Chicken-and-Rabbit Problem

A common mathematical problem goes like this:

> **A farmer had 40 chickens and rabbits altogether. He counted a total of 120 legs. Find the number of chickens and the number of rabbits the farmer had.**

There are many variations on problems of this nature. For example,

> **There are 40 cars and motorcycles altogether in a parking lot. There are only 120 wheels. Find the number of cars and the number of motorcycles in the parking lot.**

The beauty of this type of problem is the opportunity to explore a variety of problem-solving methods. Sometimes, we need to tap into our general knowledge to solve the problems.

Example 1: The farmer has 30 chickens and rabbits altogether. There are only 100 legs. Find the number of chickens and the number of rabbits that the farmer has.

Method 1: Make a Table

This method is also commonly known as the guess-and-check method. If much analytical thinking is applied, the number of steps can be greatly reduced.

Step 1: Start with half the total for each animal.
(Note that chicken has 2 legs; rabbit has 4 legs)

No. of chickens	No. of legs	No. of rabbits	No. of legs	Total no. of legs
15	30	15	60	90

Step 2: The total number of legs should be 100.

$100 - 90 = 10$ (difference in total number of legs)

$4 - 2 = 2$ (difference in the number of legs between the two animals)

$10 \div 2 = 5$ (add 5 rabbits and subtract 5 chickens to the first guess)

No. of chickens	No. of legs	No. of rabbits	No. of legs	Total no. of legs
15	30	15	60	90
10	20	20	80	100

The farmer has 10 chickens and 20 rabbits.

Method 2: Make an Assumption

This method is tricky and yet fun once you have enough practice.

If we assume all the animals were rabbits,

$$30 \times 4 = 120$$

there would be 120 legs.

As the total number of legs stated in the problem is 100,

$$120 - 100 = 20$$

there is a difference of 20 legs.

$$4 - 2 = 2$$

The difference of the number of legs between a chicken and a rabbit is 2.

$$20 \div 2 = 10$$

The farmer has 10 chickens.

$$30 - 10 = 20$$

The farmer has 20 rabbits.

Alternative Assumption

If we assume all the animals were chickens,

$$30 \times 2 = 60$$

there would be 60 legs.

$$100 - 60 = 40$$

There is a difference of 40 legs.

$$4 - 2 = 2$$

The difference of the number of legs between a chicken and a rabbit is 2.

$$40 \div 2 = 20$$

The farmer has 20 rabbits.

$$30 - 20 = 10$$

The farmer has 10 chickens.

Example 2: Samantha has 30 bills altogether. The total value of the bills is $120. Find the number of $2 bills and the number of $5 bills that Samantha has.

Method 1: Make a Table

Step 1: Start with half the total for $2 and $5 bills.

No. of $5 bills	Value	No. of $2 bills	Value	Total value
15	$75	15	$30	$105

Step 2: The total value should be $120.

$120 – $105 = $15 (difference in total value)

$5 – $2 = $3 (difference in value between $5 and $2 bills)

$15 ÷ $3 = 5 (add five $5 bills and subtract five $2 bills to the first guess)

No. of $5 bills	Value	No. of $2 bills	Value	Total value
15	$75	15	$30	$105
20	$100	10	$20	$120

Samantha has 20 $5 bills and 10 $2 bills.

Method 2: Make an Assumption

If we assume all were $5 bills,

$$30 \times \$5 = \$150$$

the total value would be $150.

$$\$150 – \$120 = \$30$$

There is a difference of $30 in the total value of money.

$$\$5 – \$2 = \$3$$
$$\$30 ÷ \$3 = 10$$

Samantha has 10 $2 bills.

$$30 – 10 = 20$$

Samantha has 20 $5 bills.

Alternative Assumption

If we assume all were $2 bills,

$$30 \times \$2 = \$60$$

the total value would be $60.

$$\$120 - \$60 = \$60$$

There is a difference of $60 in the total value of money.

$$\$5 - \$2 = \$3$$
$$\$60 \div \$3 = 20$$

Samantha has 20 $5 bills.

$$30 - 20 = 10$$

Samantha has 10 $2 bills.

Example 3: There are 24 cars and motorcycles in a parking lot. There are a total of 76 wheels. How many motorcycles are there? How many cars are there?

Method 1: Make a Table

Step 1:   Start with half the total for each vehicle.

No. of cars	No. of wheels	No. of motorcycles	No. of wheels	Total no. of wheels
12	48	12	24	72

Step 2:   The total number of wheels should be 76.

$76 - 72 = 4$ (difference in total number of wheels)

$4 - 2 = 2$ (difference in number of wheels between a car and a motorcycle)

$4 \div 2 = 2$ (add 2 cars and subtract 2 motorcycles to the first guess)

No. of cars	No. of wheels	No. of motorcycles	No. of wheels	Total no. of wheels
12	48	12	24	72
14	56	10	20	76

There are 14 cars and 10 motorcycles.

Method 2: Make an Assumption
If we assume all were cars,
$$24 \times 4 = 96$$
the total number of wheels would be 96.
$$96 - 76 = 20$$
There is a difference of 20 in the total number of wheels.
$$4 - 2 = 2$$
$$20 \div 2 = 10$$
There are 10 motorcycles.
$$24 - 10 = 14$$
There are 14 cars.

Alternative Assumption
If we assume all were motorcycles,
$$24 \times 2 = 48$$
the total number of wheels would be 48.
$$76 - 48 = 28$$
There is a difference of 28 in the total number of wheels.
$$4 - 2 = 2$$
$$28 \div 2 = 14$$
There are 14 cars.
$$24 - 14 = 10$$
There are 10 motorcycles.

© Singapore Asia Publishers Pte Ltd

978-1-62399-074-9
Singapore Math Challenge

Example 4: There were 6 questions on a math test. 5 points would be awarded for every correct answer. 2 points would be deducted for a wrong answer. If Valerie scored 23 points on the math test, how many questions did she answer correctly?

Solution:

If we assume Valerie had answered all 6 questions correctly,

$$6 \times 5 = 30$$

she would be awarded 30 points.

$$30 - 23 = 7$$

There is a difference of 7 between the full points and her score.

If Valerie had answered one question incorrectly,

$$5 + 2 = 7$$

she would lose 7 points.

$$6 - 1 = 5$$

She answered 5 questions correctly.

Example 5: There were 25 questions on a math quiz. If a question was answered correctly, 4 points would be given. Otherwise, 1 point would be deducted. If John scored 85 points on the math quiz, how many questions had he answered correctly?

Solution:

If we assume John had answered all questions correctly,

$$25 \times 4 = 100$$

he would be given 100 points.

$$100 - 85 = 15$$

There is a difference of 15 between the full points and John's score.

$$4 + 1 = 5$$

5 points would be deducted for a wrong answer.

$$15 \div 5 = 3$$

John answered 3 questions wrongly.

$$25 - 3 = 22$$

He had answered 22 questions correctly.

I. There were a total of 30 cars and motorcycles at a parking lot. There were 100 wheels in all. How many cars were there at the parking lot?

Method 1: Make a Table

No. of cars	No. of wheels	No. of motorcycles	No. of wheels	Total no. of wheels

Method 2: Make an Assumption (Assume all were motorcycles.)

2. Each adult movie ticket costs $8. Each child ticket costs $5. Sean buys 10 movie tickets altogether. He pays $74 in all. Find the number of adult movie tickets and the number of child movie tickets Sean buys.

Method 1: Make a Table

No. of adult tickets	Value	No. of child tickets	Value	Total value

Method 2: Make an Assumption (Assume either all adult tickets or all child tickets.)

3. Clifford has 30 stamps. The total value of all his stamps is $12. Find the number of 50¢ and 20¢ stamps Clifford has.

Method 1: Make a Table

No. of 50¢ stamps	Value	No. of 20¢ stamps	Value	Total value

Method 2: Make an Assumption (Assume either all 50¢ stamps or all 20¢ stamps.)

4. A spider has 8 legs and a dragonfly has 6 legs. There are 20 spiders and dragonflies altogether. There are 144 legs in all. Find the number of spiders and the number of dragonflies.

Method 1: Make a Table

No. of spiders	No. of legs	No. of dragonflies	No. of legs	Total no. of legs

Method 2: Make an Assumption (Assume either all spiders or all dragonflies.)

978-1-62399-074-9
Singapore Math Challenge

5. Natalie saves 30 bills. Her total savings is $220. How $5 bills and $10 bills does Natalie save?

Method 1: Make a Table

No. of $5 bills	Value	No. of $10 bills	Value	Total value

Method 2: Make an Assumption (Assume all are $5 bills.)

978-1-62399-074-9
Singapore Math Challenge

6. There are 30 questions on a math test. All questions must be answered. 5 points are awarded for every correct answer. 2 points will be deducted for a wrong answer. If Amy scores 122 points, how many questions does she answer correctly?

7. There were 45 questions on a science test. 4 points would be awarded for every correct answer. 2 points would be deducted for every wrong answer. All questions had to be answered. If Henry scored 150 points, how many questions had he answered wrongly?

8. For every slice of bread a child takes, an adult takes 2 slices of bread. If there are 66 adults and children in all and 99 slices of bread are taken,

  (a) how many adults are there?
  (b) how many children are there?

9. There were 100 adults and children altogether. An adult could consume 3 buns while 3 children could only finish one bun. If 100 buns were consumed, how many adults were there?

10. 56 teachers and students went for a river cruise. The seating capacity of a big boat was 8 people and the seating capacity of a small boat was 6 people. Find the number of big boats and the number of small boats.

Method 1: Make a Table

No. of big boats	No. of people	No. of small boats	No. of people	Total no. of people

Method 2: Make an Assumption (Assume either all big boats or all small boats.)

11. There are 20 questions on a math test. 8 points will be awarded for each correct answer. 4 points will be deducted for each wrong answer. All the questions must be answered. If Isabelle scores 100 points on the math test, how many questions does she answer correctly?

12. A PE teacher bought 4 identical basketballs and 5 identical volleyballs for $230. Each basketball was $8 more expensive than a volleyball. Find the cost of each basketball and each volleyball.

13. A pen cost $4 and a book cost $7. Samuel paid $64 for 10 such pens and books. Find the number of pens and the number of books he had bought.

Method 1: Make a Table

No. of pens	Cost	No. of books	Cost	Total cost

Method 2: Make an Assumption (Assume either all pens or all books.)

14. A whiteboard marker cost $3. A paintbrush cost $1. A teacher paid $28 in all for 12 paintbrushes and whiteboard markers. How many whiteboard markers and how many paintbrushes did the teacher buy?

Method 1: Make a Table

No. of whiteboard markers	Value	No. of paintbrushes	Value	Total value

Method 2: Make an Assumption (Assume either all whiteboard markers or all paintbrushes.)

Intervals

Imagine trees planted along a bike path, lamp posts placed along an expressway or stairs in an office building.

Have you ever observed the distance between these objects? Are they placed at the same distance away from each other? These objects are usually placed at regular intervals, which means that the distance between each object is the same.

In mathematics, these intervals can help us in problem-solving. For instance, we can use the intervals to find the length of the bike path, the number of lamp posts along the expressway and even the number of steps between one story and another. It is, therefore, important to take note of the number of intervals when we are dealing with problems of this nature.

The three different methods on the next two pages illustrate how the number of intervals can be calculated.

(a) If trees are planted at regular intervals with trees planted at opposite ends of the road,

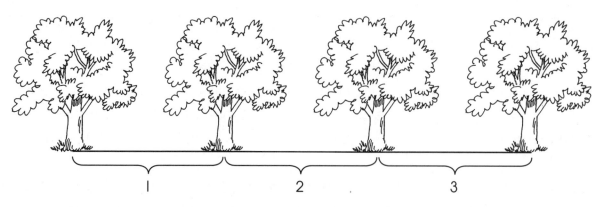

number of trees = number of intervals + 1

length of the road = number of intervals × size of the interval

number of intervals = length of the road ÷ size of the interval   OR
**   = number of trees – 1**

(b) If trees are planted at regular intervals with a tree planted at one end of the road,

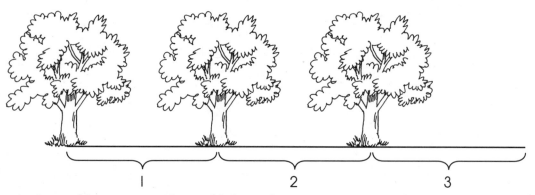

number of trees = number of intervals

length of the road = number of intervals × size of the interval

number of intervals = length of the road ÷ size of the interval

(c) If trees are planted at regular intervals without trees planted at opposite ends of the road,

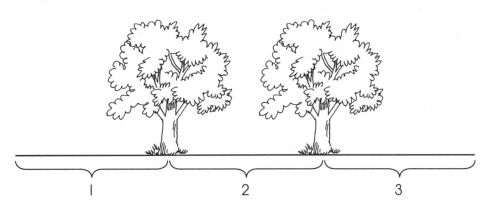

number of trees = number of intervals – 1

length of the road = number of intervals × size of the interval

number of intervals = length of the road ÷ size of the interval

Example 1: A tree is planted at every 10 meters along a stretch of road. If the stretch of road is 150 m long and the trees are planted at opposite ends of the road, how many trees are there?

Analysis: number of intervals = 150 m ÷ 10 m
$$= 15$$

Since the trees are planted at opposite ends of the road,

$$15 + 1 = 16$$

there are 16 trees.

Example 2: In a building, there are 8 steps in the staircase leading from one story to another. How many steps are there from the second to the tenth story in that building? (Assume the number of steps in each staircase is the same.)

Analysis: We must first figure out the number of intervals from the second to the tenth story.

$$10 - 2 = 8$$

There are 8 intervals from the second story to the tenth story.

8 intervals × 8 steps = 64

There are 64 steps from the second story to the tenth story in that building.

Example 3: There are 50 lamp posts along a stretch of road with lamp posts placed at opposite ends of the road. If each lamp post is 2 m away from another, how long is the road?

Analysis: number of intervals = number of lamp posts – 1
$$= 50 - 1$$
$$= 49$$

49 × 2 m = 98 m

The road is 98 m long.

Example 4: There are 21 trees planted along the road divider with trees planted at opposite ends. The trees are planted at regular intervals of 2 m. If some lamp posts are to be placed along the opposite side of the road at regular intervals of 10 m, how many lamp posts are required on the opposite side of the road if lamp posts are placed at opposite ends of the road?

Analysis: number of intervals = number of trees – 1
$$= 21 - 1$$
$$= 20$$

20 × 2 m = 40 m

The road is 40 m long.

40 m ÷ 10 m = 4

Lamp posts are placed along the opposite side of the road at 4 regular intervals.

number of lamp poles = 4 + 1 = 5

5 lamp posts are required on the opposite side of the road.

1. The stretch of road leading to Cindy's house is to be planted with some trees at regular intervals of 15 m, and trees are planted at opposite ends of the road. If the road is 900 m long, how many trees are to be planted along that stretch of road?

2. Pine trees are planted at regular intervals of 5 m along a stretch of road with pine trees planted at opposite ends of the road. If the road is 150 m long, how many pine trees are needed to be planted along the road?

3. Lamp posts are placed at regular intervals of 30 m along a 1,800-meter road. If the lamp posts are placed at opposite ends of the road, how many lamp posts are placed along the road?

4. 12 students stood in a line. If 4 pots of flowers are placed between every 2 students, how many pots of flowers are there altogether?

5. Cindy and Maurice lived on the fifth and sixth floors of an apartment building, respectively. If Cindy walked 80 steps up the staircase from the ground floor to her apartment, how many steps did Maurice walk from the ground floor to his apartment? (Assume the number of steps in each staircase is the same.)

6. Trees are planted at regular intervals along a road. If Benny takes 10 min. to walk from the first tree to the sixth tree, how long does it take for him to walk to the fifteenth tree? (Assume Benny walks at a constant rate.)

7. A grandfather clock takes 6 seconds to chime three times at 3 pm. How long does the grandfather clock take to chime 6 times at 6 pm?

8. 95 trees were planted along a road with trees planted at opposite ends of the road. Each tree was 5 m apart from the other. How long was the road?

9. Before recess, the students in Class 3D lined up in two rows. If there were 38 students in Class 3D and the distance between each student was 50 cm, what was the length of each line?

10. There are 48 students in Class 3J. All the students line up in two rows during the assembly. If the distance between each student in a row is 1 m, how long is each line?

11. 100 flags are placed at regular intervals of 6 m along a stretch of road with flags placed at opposite ends of the road. How long is the road?

12. Two buildings are 100 m apart from each other. 9 trees are planted at regular intervals **between** the two buildings. What is the distance between each tree?

13. The road leading from Betty's house to the school is planted with 79 trees at regular intervals. There are no trees in front of the school or her house. If the road is 320 m long, what is the distance between each tree?

14. The door of a PE room and the door of a science laboratory are 40 m apart. If a potted plant is placed at every 2 m **between** the two doors, how many pots of plants are there?

15. The circumference of a lake is 600 m. Trees are planted at regular intervals of 6 m around the lake. How many trees are planted around the lake?

16. Every side of a square handkerchief is embroidered with 6 flowers. A flower is embroidered on each of the four corners. How many flowers are there on the handkerchief altogether?

17. Amy used some coins to make a triangle. There were 6 coins on each side of the triangle. There was one coin on every corner. How many coins were used to make the triangle?

18. Uncle Sam went for a stroll after his dinner. He took 10 min. to walk from the first lamp post to the eleventh lamp post. At which lamp post would Uncle Sam be if he walked continuously at a constant rate for 30 min.?

19. 41 plum trees are planted along a stretch of road with trees planted at opposite ends of the road. The distance between each tree is 4 m. On the opposite side of the road, pine trees are planted at regular intervals of 5 m, with trees planted at opposite ends of the road. How many pine trees are there on this side of the road?

20. In a parade, there are 5 rows of performers. The distance between each performer in a row is 1 m. How many performers are there altogether if the length of each row of performers is 20 m?

978-1-62399-074-9
Singapore Math Challenge

Tricks in Addition and Subtraction

1. Sometimes, we break down numbers for easy addition or subtraction. Another trick is to make the numbers in addition or subtraction to be hundreds or thousands.

2. Let's learn more about the terms in addition or subtraction.

$$
\begin{array}{r}
2\ 3 \\
+\ 1\ 4 \\
\hline
3\ 7
\end{array}
$$

$2\ 3 \longrightarrow$ **addend**
$+\ 1\ 4 \longrightarrow$ **addend**
$3\ 7 \longrightarrow$ **sum**

$2\ 3 \longrightarrow$ **minuend**
$-\ 1\ 4 \longrightarrow$ **subtrahend**
$9 \longrightarrow$ **difference**

3. Below shows the properties of addition and subtraction. They are useful for easy addition or subtraction.

① $a + b - c = a - c + b$

② $a - b - c = a - c - b$

③ $a + (b - c) = a + b - c$

④ $a - (b + c) = a - b - c$

⑤ $a - (b - c) = a - b + c$

Example 1:

(a) 65 + 37 (make 100)

= 65 + 35 + 2

= 100 + 2

= 102

(b) 128 – 98 (see property 5)

= 128 – 100 + 2

= 28 + 2

= 30

(c) 643 – 97 (see property 5)

= 643 – 100 + 3

= 543 + 3

= 546

(d) 79 + 198 (see property 3)

= 79 + 200 – 2

= 279 – 2

= 277

(e) 31 + 58 + 69 (make 100)

= 31 + 69 + 58

= 100 + 58

= 158

(f) 44 + 58 + 78 (make 100)

= 40 + 58 + 2 + 78 + 2

= 40 + 60 + 80

= 180

(g) 122 + 126 + 124 + 128 + 136 + 114 (make 3 pairs of 250)

= (122 + 128) + (126 + 124) + (136 + 114)

= 250 + 250 + 250

= 750

Example 2:

(a) $200 - 89 - 11$
(see property 4)

$= 200 - (89 + 11)$

$= 200 - 100$

$= 100$

(b) $300 - 86 - 14$
(see property 4)

$= 300 - (86 + 14)$

$= 300 - 100$

$= 200$

(c) $230 - 39 - 51 - 61 - 49$
(see property 4)

$= 230 - (39 + 61 + 51 + 49)$

$= 230 - (100 + 100)$

$= 30$

(d) $453 - 34 - 35 - 65 - 66$
(see property 4)

$= 453 - (34 + 66 + 35 + 65)$

$= 453 - (100 + 100)$

$= 253$

(e) $150 - 148 + 146 - 144 + 142 - 140 + \cdots + 130 - 128$

Analysis:

$150 - 148 = 2$

$146 - 144 = 2$

$142 - 140 = 2$

We can see that every subtraction pair has a difference of 2.

How many twos are there altogether? Let's list all the minuends,

130,   134,   138,   142,   146,   150.

$2 + 2 + 2 + 2 + 2 + 2 = 12$

So, $150 - 148 + 146 - 144 + 142 - 140 + ... + 130 - 128$ is 12.

1. (a) 23 + 99

(b) 152 − 97

(c) 162 − 97

(d) 565 − 298

(e) 638 + 397

(f) 499 + 127

(g) 645 − 98

(h) 533 − 199

(i) 285 + 297

(j) 424 − 196

(k) 43 + 99 + 58

(l) 56 + 87 + 77

(m) 74 + 75 + 28

(n) 27 + 86 + 63 + 14

(o) 323 + 677 + 92 + 108

(p) 167 + 355 + 345 + 133

(q) $9,999 + 999 + 99 + 9$

(r) $18 + 28 + 38 + 48 + 58$

(s) $9,997 + 4 + 99 + 998 + 3 + 9$

(t) $74 + 75 + 77 + 80 + 82 + 85$

(u) $299,999 + 29,999 + 2,999 + 299 + 29$

(v) $133 + 135 + 140 + 147 + 145 + 142 + 138$

978-1-62399-074-9
Singapore Math Challenge

2. (a) 420 – 102 – 98

(b) 240 – 104 – 96

(c) 325 – 10 – 20 – 80 – 90

(d) 400 – 90 – 80 – 20 – 10 – 5

(e) 235 – 15 – 25 – 75 – 85

(f) 200 – 1 – 2 – 3 – 4 – 5

(g) $120 - 117 + 116 - 113 + 112 - 109 + \ldots + 100 - 97$

(h) $145 - 141 + 140 - 136 + 135 - 131 + \ldots + 95 - 91$

(i) $800 - 10 - 20 - 30 - 40 - 50 - 60 - 70 - 80 - 90$

3. (a) 375 + 286 + 125 + 714

(b) 728 + 140 + 272

(c) 37 + 97 + 3,997 + 99

(d) 71 + 69 + 68 + 73 + 74

(e) 1,897 + 128 – 597

(f) 728 – (28 + 320)

(g) 1,290 – 164 – 736

(h) 1,330 – 288 – 342

978-1-62399-074-9
Singapore Math Challenge

(i) 843 + 78 – 43

(j) 528 – (186 + 328)

(k) 564 – (387 – 136)

(l) 847 – 578 + 398 – 222

(m) 936 – 867 – 99 + 267

(n) 33 + 87 + 67 + 13

(o) 96 + 103 + 97 + 104 + 101 + 99

978-1-62399-074-9
Singapore Math Challenge

(p) 23 + 56 + 77 + 18 + 44 + 82

(q) 9 + 99 + 999 + 9,999

(r) 8 + 98 + 998 + 9,998

(s) 464 – 548 + 99 + 348

(t) 537 – (543 – 163) – 57

(u) 713 – (513 – 229)

(v) 850 – 486 – 114

(w) 46 + 37 + 54 + 63

(x) 947 + (372 – 447) – 572

(y) 989 – 675 – 189

(z) 583 – 297 – 183

4. 360 – 357 + 354 – 351 + ⋯ + 300 – 297

978-1-62399-074-9
Singapore Math Challenge

Tricks in Multiplication and Division

Here are some tricks on how to multiply or divide numbers at a faster rate.

1. Laws of Multiplication

Commutative Law of Multiplication	$a \times b = b \times a$
Associative Law of Multiplication	$(a \times b) \times c = a \times (b \times c)$
Distributive Law of Multiplication	$a \times (b + c) = a \times b + a \times c$
	$a \times (b - c) = a \times b - a \times c$

2. Multiplication tables of 10, 100 and 1,000

Sometimes, it helps us to work faster in multiplication and division if we are familiar with the multipliers and multiplicands of 10, 100 and 1,000.

multiplier × multiplicand = product

$2 \times 5 = 10$

$10 \times 10 = 100$ $20 \times 5 = 100$ $25 \times 4 = 100$

$10 \times 100 = 1,000$ $20 \times 50 = 1,000$ $25 \times 40 = 1,000$

$125 \times 8 = 1,000$ $200 \times 5 = 1,000$ $250 \times 4 = 1,000$

$500 \times 2 = 1,000$

3. Prime Factorization

A prime number is a number that can only be divided by the number itself and 1. 2, 3, 5, 7, 11, 13 and 17 are examples of prime numbers.

4. Multiplication of 11 and 101

$$45 \times 11 = 45 + (45 \times 10)$$
$$= 45 + 450$$
$$= 495$$

```
    4 5
+ 4 5 0
───────
  4 9 5
```

To multiply a number by 11, just add the number to the product of that number and 10.

$$63 \times 101 = 6,363$$
$$59 \times 101 = 5,959$$

When a two-digit number is multiplied by 101, the four-digit product is simply the repeat of the two digits.

5. Unusual Multiplication Pattern

If the sum of the digits in the ones places of two 2-digit numbers is 10 and their digits in the tens places are the same, you can work out the product using the method shown below.

$$72 \times 78$$

Step 1:   To find the first two digits of the product,

digit in the tens place × (digit in the tens place + 1)

$$7 \times (7 + 1) = 7 \times 8 = 56$$

Step 2:   To find the last two digits of the product,

digit in the ones place of the first number × digit in the ones place of the second number

$$2 \times 8 = 16$$
$$72 \times 78 = 5,616$$

97   978-1-62399-074-9
Singapore Math Challenge

Example 1:

(a)　$2 \times 5 \times 4 \times 25$
　　$= 10 \times 100$
　　$= 1{,}000$

(b)　$26 \times 5 \times 8 \times 125$
　　$= 13 \times (2 \times 5) \times (8 \times 125)$
　　$= 13 \times 10 \times 1{,}000$
　　$= 13 \times 10{,}000$
　　$= 130{,}000$

(c)　$125 \times 8 \times 25 \times 4$
　　$= 1{,}000 \times 100$
　　$= 100{,}000$

(d)　88×125
　　$= 11 \times (8 \times 125)$
　　$= 11 \times 1{,}000$
　　$= 11{,}000$

(e)　44×25
　　$= 11 \times (4 \times 25)$
　　$= 11 \times 100$
　　$= 1{,}100$

(f)　25×28
　　$= (25 \times 4) \times 7$
　　$= 100 \times 7$
　　$= 700$

(g)　$50 \times 20 \times 8 \times 125$
　　$5 \times 10 \times 2 \times 10 \times 8 \times 125$
　　$= (5 \times 2) \times (10 \times 10) \times (8 \times 125)$
　　$= 10 \times 100 \times 1{,}000$
　　$= 1{,}000{,}000$

Example 2-1: Find the prime factors of the following numbers.

(a) 15
$= 3 \times 5$

(b) 45
$= 5 \times 9$
$= 5 \times 3 \times 3$

(c) 32
$= 4 \times 8$
$= 2 \times 2 \times 2 \times 2 \times 2$

(d) 78
$= 39 \times 2$
$= 13 \times 3 \times 2$

(e) 180
$= 60 \times 3$
$= 20 \times 3 \times 3$
$= 4 \times 5 \times 3 \times 3$
$= 2 \times 2 \times 5 \times 3 \times 3$

(f) 210
$= 3 \times 70$
$= 3 \times 2 \times 35$
$= 3 \times 2 \times 5 \times 7$

© Singapore Asia Publishers Pte Ltd

978-1-62399-074-9
Singapore Math Challenge

Example 2-2: Find the prime factors of the following number using a tree diagram.

(a)   80

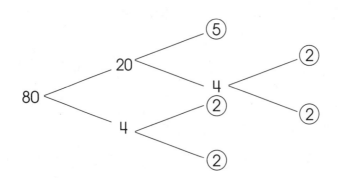

$80 = 2 \times 2 \times 2 \times 2 \times 5$

We can also start off the prime factorization with another set of numbers.

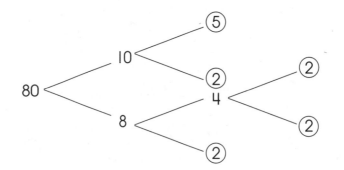

The result will still be the same.

$80 = 2 \times 2 \times 2 \times 2 \times 5$

Example 3:

(a) $5 \times 17 + 5 \times 73$
$= 5 \times (17 + 73)$
$= 5 \times 90$
$= 450$

(b) $23 \times 4 + 23 \times 6$
$= 23 \times (4 + 6)$
$= 23 \times 10$
$= 230$

(c) $43 \times 25 + 57 \times 25$
$= (43 + 57) \times 25$
$= 100 \times 25$
$= 2,500$

(d) $45 \div 13 + 345 \div 13$
$= (45 + 345) \div 13$
$= 390 \div 13$
$= 30$

(e) 25×101
$= 25 \times (100 + 1)$
$= 25 \times 100 + 25 \times 1$
$= 2,500 + 25$
$= 2,525$

(f) 37×98
$= 37 \times (100 - 2)$
$= (37 \times 100) - (37 \times 2)$
$= 3,700 - 74$
$= 3,626$

(g) $4 \times (28 \times 25 + 72 \times 25)$
$= (4 \times 25) \times 28 + (4 \times 25) \times 72$
$= 100 \times 28 + 100 \times 72$
$= 100 \times (28 + 72)$
$= 100 \times 100$
$= 10,000$

(h) $8 \times (86 \times 125 + 14 \times 125)$
$= (8 \times 125) \times 86 + (8 \times 125) \times 14$
$= 1,000 \times 86 + 1,000 \times 14$
$= 1,000 \times (86 + 14)$
$= 1,000 \times 100$
$= 100,000$

Example 4-1:

(a)   25 × 11

```
      2 5
  +  2 5 0
  ─────────
     2 7 5
```

(b)   35 × 11

```
      3 5
  +  3 5 0
  ─────────
     3 8 5
```

(c)   89 × 11

```
      8 9
  +  8 9 0
  ─────────
     9 7 9
```

(d)   55 × 11

```
      5 5
  +  5 5 0
  ─────────
     6 0 5
```

Example 4-2:

(a)   25 × 101 = 2,525

(b)   88 × 101 = 8,888

Example 5:

(a) 63×67

$6 \times (6 + 1) = 42$

$3 \times 7 = 21$

$63 \times 67 = 4{,}221$

(b) 54×56

$5 \times (5 + 1) = 30$

$4 \times 6 = 24$

$54 \times 56 = 3{,}024$

(c) 36×34

$3 \times (3 + 1) = 12$

$6 \times 4 = 24$

$36 \times 34 = 1{,}224$

(d) 82×88

$8 \times (8 + 1) = 72$

$2 \times 8 = 16$

$82 \times 88 = 7{,}216$

978-1-62399-074-9
Singapore Math Challenge

Name ______________________ Date ____________

1. (a) $14 \times 25 \times 4$

(b) $4 \times 17 \times 25$

(c) $25 \times 32 \times 125$

(d) $125 \times 25 \times 4$

(e) 56×125

(f) 125×72

978-1-62399-074-9

(g) $64 \times 5 \times 25 \times 125$

(h) $56 \times 25 \times 2 \times 5$

(i) $25 \times 16 \times 125 \times 4 \times 5$

(j) $25 \times 64 \times 125 \times 25$

(k) $25 \times 24 \times 8 \times 125$

(l) $25 \times 40 \times 125 \times 8$

2-1. Find the prime factors of the following.

(a) 24

(b) 36

(c) 27

(d) 44

(e) 42

(f) 56

(g) 33

(h) 64

(i) 48

(j) 99

2-2. Find the prime factors of the following numbers using a tree diagram.

(a) 90

(b) 175

(c) 180

(d) 225

978-1-62399-074-9
Singapore Math Challenge

3. (a) $7 \times 14 + 7 \times 86$

(b) $65 \div 11 + 56 \div 11$

(c) $24 \times 23 + 24 \times 77$

(d) $31 \times 84 + 31 \times 16$

(e) $58 \div 12 + 86 \div 12$

(f) $100 \div 14 + 96 \div 14$

(g) 35×202

(h) 45×98

(i) 72×101

(j) 38×99

(k) 33×97

(l) 83×99

(m) $4 \times (72 \times 25 + 28 \times 25)$

(n) $(110 + 25 - 9) \times 8$

978-1-62399-074-9
Singapore Math Challenge

(o) $125 \times (84 \times 8 + 16 \times 8)$

(p) $8 \times (98 - 48 + 74)$

(q) $25 \times (28 \times 4 + 72 \times 4)$

(r) $25 \times 73 + 50 \times 73 + 25 \times 73$

(s) $74 + 5 \times 740 + 49 \times 74$

(t) $81 + 5 \times 810 + 49 \times 81$

4. (a) 34×11

(b) 45×11

(c) 27×11

(d) 37×11

(e) 345×11

(f) 123×11

(g) 426×11

(h) 286×11

978-1-62399-074-9
Singapore Math Challenge

(i) 14 × 101

(j) 67 × 101

(k) 23 × 101

(l) 45 × 101

(m) 82 × 101

(n) 98 × 101

(o) 63 × 101

(p) 76 × 101

5. (a) 43×47 **(b)** 54×56

(c) 52×58 **(d)** 66×64

(e) 73×77 **(f)** 89×81

(g) 92×98 **(h)** 57×53

(i) 42×48

(j) 85×85

(k) 44×46

(l) 74×76

Logic

To solve problems involving logic, two strategies are often used.

The first strategy is to assume that a condition is true. Then, we will check if our assumption is correct in the later part of the problem-solving.

The next strategy is to eliminate all the conditions that cannot be true.

In addition, creating a table or drawing helps us analyze the problem and find the solution in a systematic way.

978-1-62399-074-9
Singapore Math Challenge

Example 1: The places of birth of Cindy, Eleanor and Daisy are Indonesia, Thailand and Brunei, but not in that order.

> **Cindy has never been to Indonesia.**
>
> **Eleanor was not born in Indonesia.**
>
> **Eleanor was not born in Brunei.**

> Can you find out their places of birth?

Solution:

Use a table to help us sort out the information.

	Indonesia	Thailand	Brunei
Cindy	✗		
Eleanor	✗		✗
Daisy			

From the above table, it is clear that Eleanor was born in Thailand and Daisy was born in Indonesia.

Since Cindy was not born in Indonesia or Thailand, her place of birth must be Brunei.

Example 2: Jolene, Charlie and Natalie were classmates. One of them cleaned up the classroom one day while there was nobody around. Below are their replies when the teacher questioned about who cleaned up the classroom.

> **Jolene : Charlie cleaned the classroom.**
> **Charlie : I did not do it!**
> **Natalie : Neither did I!**

If one of them was telling the truth, find out who cleaned up the classroom.

Solution:

Use tables to make assumptions.

If Jolene cleaned up the classroom,

Table 1	Truth	Lie
Jolene		✓
Charlie	✓	
Natalie	✓	

If Charlie cleaned up the classroom,

Table 2	Truth	Lie
Jolene	✓	
Charlie		✓
Natalie	✓	

If Natalie cleaned up the classroom,

Table 3	Truth	Lie
Jolene		✓
Charlie	✓	
Natalie		✓

If one of them was telling the truth, table 3 is likely to be the correct assumption. So, Natalie was the one who cleaned up the classroom.

Example 3: ❖ + ○ = 54

    ❖ = ○ + ○ + ○ + ○ + ○

    Find the values of each ❖ and each ○.

Solution:

    6○ = 54

    ○ = 54 ÷ 6 = 9

    ❖ = 5 × 9 = 45

Example 4: ❖ = □ + □ + □ + □ + □

    ❖ × □ = 20

    Find the values of each ❖ and each □.

Solution:

    ❖ = 5 × □

    5 × □ × □ = 20

    □ × □ = 20 ÷ 5 = 4

    □ × □ = 4

    □ = 2

    ❖ = 5 × 2 = 10

Example 5: Four teams are competing against each other for District Volleyball Championship. Every team must play exactly once against each of the other three teams. So far, Team A has played 3 matches, Team B has played 2 matches and Team D has played 1 match. How many match(es) has Team C played?

Solution:

Use a drawing to help us solve this problem. The lines used in the drawing represent the number of matches each team has played.

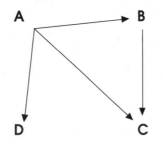

Based on the above drawing, we can make two conclusions.

(1) Team A has played 3 matches. This means that it has played against Team B, Team C and Team D.

(2) Team B has played 2 matches. Besides playing against Team A, it could have only played against Team C as Team D has played only 1 match against Team A.

So, Team C has played 2 matches.

978-1-62399-074-9
Singapore Math Challenge

1. Zachary, Nicholas and Philip are old classmates. During a recent gathering, they told each other about their occupations. Among them, there is an accountant, a bus driver and a manager.

Below are the hints about their occupations.

Philip is older than the accountant.
Zachary's age is not the same as the bus driver.
The bus driver is younger than Nicholas.

Can you find out their occupations?

	Zachary	Nicholas	Philip
accountant			
bus driver			
manager			

2. Among Kim and two other friends, Bernice is the lightest and Sabrina is the heaviest. The table below shows the total weight of two girls weighing themselves.

1st reading	45 kg
2nd reading	55 kg
3rd reading	50 kg

Find the weight of each girl.

3. $\square + \bigcirc = 64$

$\square = \bigcirc + \bigcirc + \bigcirc + \bigcirc + \bigcirc + \bigcirc + \bigcirc$

Find the values of each $\square$ and each $\bigcirc$.

4. $\triangle = \bigcirc + \bigcirc + \bigcirc + \bigcirc + \bigcirc$

$\triangle \times \bigcirc = 45$

Find the values of each $\bigcirc$ and each $\triangle$.

5. Among Calvin, Leon and Henry, one works as a doctor, and the other two men work as a teacher and an army officer.
Below are the hints about their jobs.

Henry is older than the army officer.
Calvin is not of the same age as the teacher.
The teacher is younger than Leon.

Find Calvin's, Leon's and Henry's jobs.

	Calvin	Leon	Henry
doctor			
teacher			
army officer			

6. There are five people, A, B, C, D and E.
Below is some information about these five people.

 A is older than B.
 C is younger than E but older than D.
 D is older than B.
 E is younger than A.

Rank the five people, starting with the youngest.

7. Two suspects, A and B, are on trial for shoplifting. Four witnesses are called in during the trial. Below are the witnesses' testimonies.

1st **witness :** I know A is innocent!

2nd **witness :** I know B is innocent!

3rd **witness :** The facts presented by the first and second witnesses are true.

4th **witness :** I am very certain that the third witness is lying!

If only the 4th witness is telling the truth, which suspect(s) is/are guilty of shoplifting?

8. Mr. Wood and Mr. Smith each have two children under 9 years old. Below is some information about their children.

Mike is 3 years younger than his brother.
Royston is the oldest among the four children.
Sean's age is half of Mr. Wood's child's age.
Jack is 1 year older than Mr. Smith's younger child.
Each family had only one child three years ago.

Each child is a different age. Can you list the children's ages and match them with their family members?

9. A chocolate cake was missing from the refrigerator. Mom suspected that one of the children took the chocolate cake. Below are their replies when Mom questioned each of them.

> **Sean: I did not take the chocolate cake.**
> **Cindy: I didn't even know you had bought a cake!**
> **Jack: Sean took the chocolate cake!**

If only one of them was telling the truth, who took the chocolate cake?

If Sean took the chocolate cake,

	Truth	Lie
Sean		
Cindy		
Jack		

If Cindy took the chocolate cake,

	Truth	Lie
Sean		
Cindy		
Jack		

If Jack took the chocolate cake,

	Truth	Lie
Sean		
Cindy		
Jack		

978-1-62399-074-9
Singapore Math Challenge

10. If   □ + ✱ = 11,

✤ + □ = 9,

✱ + ✤ = 10.

Find the values of each □, each ✱ and each ✤ .

11. If   ○ + △ = 22,

✤ + ○ = 18,

△ + ✤ = 20.

Find the values of each ○, each △ and each ✤ .

12. In a school, there are four Grade 5 classes. In each class, two of the students are elected as class helpers. Meetings for class helpers in the school are held every two weeks. Only one helper from each class is required to attend.

A, B, C and D attended the first meeting.

E, B, F and D attended the second meeting.

A, E, B, and G attended the third meeting.

If H has not attended any meetings, who are the two helpers in each class?

	A	B	C	D	E	F	G	H
first meeting								
second meeting								
third meeting								

13. Mother baked a blueberry pie in the morning. By afternoon, half of the pie was gone. Below are the kids' replies when she questioned them about who had taken the pie without asking her.

Jacelyn: Kate took the pie!
Kate: I did not eat the pie!
Polly: I did not touch the pie!

If only one of the kids was telling the truth, who took half of the blueberry pie?

If Jacelyn took the blueberry pie,

	Truth	Lie
Jacelyn		
Kate		
Polly		

If Kate took the blueberry pie,

	Truth	Lie
Jacelyn		
Kate		
Polly		

If Polly took the blueberry pie,

	Truth	Lie
Jacelyn		
Kate		
Polly		

14. $\square + \square + \clubsuit + \clubsuit + \clubsuit = 36$

$\square + \square + \square + \clubsuit + \clubsuit + \clubsuit + \clubsuit = 50$

Find the values of each $\square$ and each $\clubsuit$.

15. $\bigcirc + \bigcirc + \bigcirc + \square + \square + \square + \square = 43$

$\bigcirc + \bigcirc + \bigcirc + \bigcirc + \square + \square + \square + \square + \square = 55$

Find the values of each $\bigcirc$ and each $\square$.

978-1-62399-074-9
Singapore Math Challenge

16. A few years ago, there were four Mondays and four Fridays in the month of January. On which day in that year was January 1st?

Sun.	Mon.	Tues.	Wed.	Thurs.	Fri.	Sat.

17. Sean, Karen, Susan and Kelvin are comparing their heights.

> **Sean:**   I am the tallest.
> **Karen:** I am not the shortest.
> **Susan:** I am not as tall as Sean but someone is shorter than me.
> **Kelvin:** I am the shortest.

If one of them is lying, can you rank their heights starting with the tallest?

978-1-62399-074-9
Singapore Math Challenge

18. Five teams take part in a basketball league. Each team has to play exactly one game against every other team. So far, Team A has played 4 games and Team B has played 3 games. If Team D and Team E have each played 2 games, how many game(s) might Team C have played?

19. When Mr. Simon found out that someone had broken his window, he wanted to catch the culprit. Below are the children's replies when he questioned them.

Bob: **Joe did it!**
Katy: **I didn't even know that the window was broken.**
Joe: **Bob is lying!**

If only one child was telling the truth, who actually broke the window?

If Bob broke the window,

	Truth	Lie
Bob		
Katy		
Joe		

If Katy broke the window,

	Truth	Lie
Bob		
Katy		
Joe		

If Joe broke the window,

	Truth	Lie
Bob		
Katy		
Joe		

978-1-62399-074-9
Singapore Math Challenge

20. A paper airplane flew right onto the back of Miss Kay as she was writing on the whiteboard. The suspects were narrowed down to 3 students who were brought to the principal.

Below are the students' replies when they were questioned by the principal.

> **Joshua:** **I did not fly the paper airplane.**
> **Paul:** **Neither did I!**
> **James:** **Joshua did it!**

If only one of them was telling the truth, who flew the paper airplane?

If Joshua flew the paper airplane,

	Truth	Lie
Joshua		
Paul		
James		

If Paul flew the paper airplane,

	Truth	Lie
Joshua		
Paul		
James		

If James flew the paper airplane,

	Truth	Lie
Joshua		
Paul		
James		

21. The number tags 22, 23, 24 and 25 are given out to four runners in a 3,000-meter race. These four runners are from France, America, Romania and Russia. Four spectators make the following comments.

Spectator A: Number 22 is French. Number 23 is American.
Spectator B: Number 23 is Romanian. Number 22 is Russian.
Spectator C: Number 24 is American. Number 25 is Romanian.
Spectator D: Number 24 is Romanian. Number 25 is Russian.

If each of the spectators makes only one correct guess in his or her comments, what are the number tags of each runner?

	French	American	Russian	Romanian
Number 22				
Number 23				
Number 24				
Number 25				

978-1-62399-074-9
Singapore Math Challenge

22. A few years ago, there were 4 Saturdays and 4 Wednesdays in the month of March. On which day in that year was March 10th?

Sun.	Mon.	Tues.	Wed.	Thurs.	Fri.	Sat.

Speed: Catching Up

Speed is ubiquitous in our everyday lives. Consider:

> What was the driving speed of the school bus you took this morning?
>
> At what speed does your father always drive?
>
> How fast can you swim?
>
> How many meters can you walk in one minute?
>
> How fast does a motorboat travel down a canal?

Can you find the answers to the above questions?

The formulas for speed-related problems are:

Speed = **Distance ÷ Time**

Distance = **Speed × Time**

Time = **Distance ÷ Speed**

Usually, we use drawings to help us solve speed-related problems. These drawings help us analyze the situation and have a clearer picture of the problems.

978-1-62399-074-9
Singapore Math Challenge

Example 1: If I can cover a distance of 100 meters per minute on foot, how many minutes does it take for me to cover a distance of 800 meters?

$$100 \text{ m} \quad \rightarrow \quad 1 \text{ min.}$$
$$800 \text{ m} \quad \rightarrow \quad 800 \div 100 = 8 \text{ min.}$$

It takes 8 minutes for me to cover a distance of 800 meters.

Example 2: Jonathan's school is 630 meters away from his house. If he walks at a speed of 70 meters per minute, how long does it take for him to reach his school?

$$70 \text{ m} \quad \rightarrow \quad 1 \text{ min.}$$
$$630 \text{ m} \quad \rightarrow \quad 630 \div 70 = 9 \text{ min.}$$

It takes 9 minutes for him to reach his school.

Example 3: Andy can jog a distance of 60 meters in 12 seconds. How long does it take for him to cover a 400-meter jogging track?

$$12 \text{ sec.} \quad \rightarrow \quad 60 \text{ m}$$
$$1 \text{ sec.} \quad \rightarrow \quad 60 \div 12 = 5 \text{ m}$$
$$400 \div 5 = 80 \text{ sec.}$$

It takes 80 seconds for him to cover a 400-meter jogging track.

Example 4: Natalie's father started jogging in the park at a speed of 120 meters per minute. 5 minutes later, Natalie began to bicycle along the same route at 220 meters per minute. How long would Natalie take to catch up with her father?

Method 1: Make A List

Time	Distance covered by her father	Distance covered by Natalie	How far was her father ahead of Natalie?
5th min.	5 × 120 = 600 m	0 m	600 m
6th min.	6 × 120 = 720 m	1 × 220 = 220 m	500 m
7th min.	7 × 120 = 840 m	2 × 220 = 440 m	400 m
8th min.	8 × 120 = 960 m	3 × 220 = 660 m	300 m
9th min.	9 × 120 = 1,080 m	4 × 220 = 880 m	200 m
10th min.	10 × 120 = 1,200 m	5 × 220 = 1,100 m	100 m
11th min.	11 × 120 = 1,320 m	6 × 220 = 1,320 m	0 m

Natalie would take 6 minutes to catch up with her father.

Method 2: Solve By Reasoning

$$5 \text{ min.} \times 120 \text{ m} = 600 \text{ m}$$

Her father was ahead of Natalie by 600 m when she just started to bicycle.

$$220 \text{ m} - 120 \text{ m} = 100 \text{ m}$$

The difference between Natalie's bicycling speed and her father's jogging speed was 100 m.

$$600 \text{ m} \div 100 \text{ m} = 6 \text{ min.}$$

So, Natalie would take 6 minutes to catch up with her father.

1. Melvin can run at a speed of 150 meters per minute. How long does it take for him to run a distance of 900 meters?

2. Cindy can bicycle at a speed of 120 meters per minute. How far can she bicycle in 5 minutes?

3. Adrian can jog at a speed of 60 meters every 12 seconds. How long does he take to jog 400 meters?

4. Benny can cover a distance of 800 meters on foot in 5 minutes. How long does it take for him to cover a distance of 1,280 meters?

5. A swimmer swims at a speed of 50 meters in 60 seconds. How far can he cover in 240 seconds if he continues to swim at the same speed?

6. Diana and Elaine were jogging in the park. They started jogging from the same point but at different speeds. Diana's speed was 80 meters per minute and Elaine's speed was 70 meters per minute. How far was Elaine behind Diana after 8 minutes?

7. Joe biked at a speed of 200 meters per minute. His brother biked at a speed of 180 meters per minute. If they started biking from the same place, how far was Joe ahead of his brother after 10 minutes? (Assume their speed to be the same throughout the 10 minutes.)

8. A cat spotted a mouse that was 20 m away. If the cat could run at a speed of 4 meters per second and the rat ran at a speed of 2 meters per second, how long would the cat take to catch the rat?

9. A rabbit is 50 meters in front of a hound. The rabbit can run at a speed of 7 meters per second. The hound can run at a speed of 12 meters per second. How long does the hound take to catch up with the rabbit?

10. A jaguar spotted its prey that was 100 meters away. It started to dash toward the prey at a speed of 15 meters per second. The prey could only run at a speed of 10 meters per second. How long would the jaguar take to catch its prey?

11. Mr. Thomas started jogging at a speed of 200 meters per minute in a park. Five minutes later, his daughter, Jacklyn, started biking at a speed of 400 meters per minute in the same park. How long would Jacklyn take to catch up with her dad?

Method 1: Make A List

Time	Distance traveled by Mr. Thomas	Distance traveled by Jacklyn	Distance between them
5th min.	200 m/min. × 5 = 1,000 m	0 m	1,000 m

Method 2: Solve By Reasoning

12. A train left City A for City B at a speed of 60 km/h. Five hours later, an express train started its journey at a speed of 120 km/h. How long did the express train take to catch up with the first train if each train continued to travel at its own speed throughout the journey?

Method 1: Make A List

Time	Distance traveled by the first train	Distance traveled by the express train	Distance between the two trains

Method 2: Solve By Reasoning

13. Sam can reach his destination, which is 560 km away, on time if he drives at a speed of 70 km/h. By how much should he increase his driving speed if he wants to arrive at the destination an hour early?

14. A train was scheduled to arrive in Town B at 3 pm if it traveled at 50 kilometers per hour and started its journey at 9 am. The train could only start the journey at 10 am due to an engine problem. What was the speed that the train had to travel in order to arrive in Town B at 3 pm?

15. A train left Town A for Town B at 8 am at a speed of 60 km/h. The scheduled time of arrival was 4 pm. If the train was late by 2 hours, what would be its actual speed for the journey?

16. Cindy walks to school at 7 am every morning. If her walking speed is 40 meters per minute, she will reach the school at 7:10 am. Cindy woke up late one morning and started walking to school at 7:04 am. If she reached the school at 7:12 am, at what speed did she walk?

17. Every morning, Samuel walks to school at a speed of 50 m/min. John's walking speed to the school is 60 m/min. The school is 300 m away from their home.

    (a) How long does each of them take to walk to school?

    (b) At what time will each of them reach the school if Samuel and John start to walk to school at 7 am and 7:01 am respectively?

18. A running track is 400 meters. Alex can run 400 meters in one minute. William can run 320 meters in one minute. If Alex starts to run one minute after William has started running, how long has William been running when Alex catches up with him?

978-1-62399-074-9
Singapore Math Challenge

19. John walks to school every morning. If John walks at a speed of 50 meters per minute, he will be 5 minutes late. If he walks at a speed of 70 meters per minute, he will reach the school just 5 minutes before the bell rings. How far away is the school from John's house?

20. Every morning, Alice walks to school. If she walks at a speed of 60 meters per minute, she will be 4 minutes late. If she walks at a speed of 80 meters per minute, she will reach the school just 4 minutes before the bell rings. How far away is the school from Alice's house?

Speed: Encountering

Example 1: Charles and his brother were 250 meters apart in the park. They began walking toward each other at a speed of 25 meters per minute and 30 meters per minute respectively. How far were they apart after 4 minutes?

Solution:

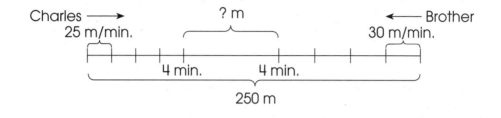

Distance = Speed × Time

$$25 \text{ m/min.} \times 4 \text{ min.} = 100 \text{ m}$$

Charles walked 100 m in 4 min.

$$30 \text{ m/min.} \times 4 \text{ min.} = 120 \text{ m}$$

His brother walked 120 m in 4 min.

$$100 \text{ m} + 120 \text{ m} = 220 \text{ m}$$

$$250 \text{ m} - 220 \text{ m} = 30 \text{ m}$$

They were 30 m apart after 4 minutes.

Example 2: In a park, Cindy and Betty set off biking from the same place but in opposite directions. Cindy biked at a speed of 100 m/min. and Betty biked at 120 m/min. How far were they apart after 5 minutes?

Solution:

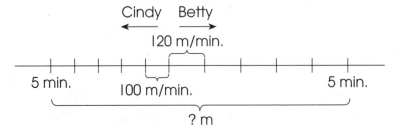

100 m/min. × 5 min. = 500 m (distance traveled by Cindy)

120 m/min. × 5 min. = 600 m (distance traveled by Betty)

500 m + 600 m = 1,100 m

They were 1,100 m apart after 5 minutes.

Example 3: Diana walked toward the library at a speed of 35 m/min. At the same time, her sister, Elaine, returned from the library at a walking speed of 45 m/min. If they met 140 m from their house, how far was the library from their house?

Solution:

Let us simplify the problem and consider Diana alone first.

1 min. → 35 m

140 m ÷ 35 m = 4 min.

Diana met her sister after walking for 4 min. Elaine walked for 4 min., too.

45 m/min. × 4 min. = 180 m (distance traveled by Elaine)

140 m + 180 m = 320 m

The library was 320 m from their house.

Example 4: A train is 150 m long. If it travels at 15 m/sec., how long does it take for the train to pass through a tunnel that is 300 m long?

Solution:

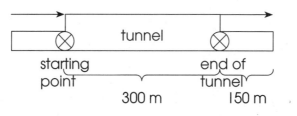

In order to pass through the tunnel, the train has to travel a distance of 300 m and another 150 m (length of the train) to be out of the tunnel.

300 m + 150 m = 450 m

So, the train travels a total distance of 450 m.

Time = Distance ÷ Speed
      = 450 m ÷ 15 m/sec.
      = 30 sec.

It takes 30 seconds for the train to pass through a tunnel that is 300 m long.

1. In the park, Natalie and her sister were 500 m apart at first. They began walking toward each other at the same time. Natalie and her sister's walking speeds were 40 m/min. and 50 m/min. respectively. How far were they apart after 5 minutes?

2. Travis lives 2,500 m away from Zane. Last Saturday, they biked toward each other's houses at the same time. Travis biked at a speed of 220 m/min. and Zane cycled at a speed of 240 m/min. How far were they apart after 5 minutes?

3. Adeline lives 500 m away from Beatrice's house. Adeline can walk at 60 m/min. which is 10 m/min. faster than Beatrice. How far are they apart after 4 minutes if both girls start walking toward each other's houses at the same time?

4. After school, Sean walked east toward the direction of his house at a speed of 40 m/min. Richard walked in the opposite direction at a speed of 50 m/min. How far were they away from each other after 4 minutes?

5. In a park, John and Mark set off biking from the same place but in opposite directions. John biked at a speed of 250 m/min. and Mark biked at a speed of 300 m/min. How far were they apart after 4 minutes?

6. A car traveled from Town A at a speed of 65 km/h toward Town B. Another car traveled at a speed of 60 km/h from Town B toward Town A at the same time. The two cars met after 8 hours. How far was Town B from Town A?

7. Town X and Town Y are 390 km apart. A car travels from Town X at 70 km/h. At the same time, a van starts to travel at 60 km/h from Town Y. Where and when do the car and the van pass each other?

8. A train left Town A for Town B at a speed of 36 km/h. Another train left Town B for Town A at a speed of 64 km/h. If the two towns were 900 km apart, when did the two trains meet?

9. Sunshine Town and Riverview Town were 2,000 km apart. Car A left Sunshine Town for Riverview Town. At the same time, car B left Riverview Town for Sunshine Town. The two cars met 10 hours later. If car A was faster than car B by 20 km/h, what were the driving speeds of the two cars?

10. George City and Meadow City are 980 km apart. Two vans travel toward each other from the two cities. The faster van travels at a speed of 50 km/h. If the two vans meet each other 10 hours later, what is the speed of the slower van?

11. Sean's house was 1,600 m away from a garden. After Sean walked toward the garden for 5 minutes, Charles biked toward Sean's house from the garden at a speed of 220 m/min. If they met each other 10 minutes later, what was Sean's walking speed?

12. Town Y and Town Z were 512 km apart. Car A left Town Y for Town Z at a speed of 32 km/h. An hour later, car B left Town Z for Town Y at twice car A's speed. How long would it take for the two cars to pass each other after car B left Town Z?

13. The library was 700 m away from my house. My brother walked at a speed of 30 m/min. from the library. At the same time, I walked from my house toward the library at a speed of 40 m/min. When and at what distance from my house would I meet my brother?

14. I walked toward a shopping mall at a speed of 50 m/min. At the same time, my brother returned from the shopping mall at a walking speed of 60 m/min. We met 250 m away from home. How far was the shopping mall from my house?

15. Train A traveled from Town C to Town D at a speed of 60 km/h. At the same time, Train B traveled from Town D to Town C but at a speed 20 km/h faster than Train A. If the two trains met 6 hours later, how far was Town D from Town C?

16. Charles walked from his house toward Jonathan's house at a speed of 20 m/min. Jonathan walked from his house toward Charles's house at a speed of 30 m/min. at the same time. They met each other 100 m away from Charles's house. How far was Jonathan's house from Charles's?

17. A car traveled at a speed of 70 km/h toward Valley Town from Richmond Town. At the same time, another car traveled from Valley Town at a speed of 80 km/h toward Richmond Town. The two cars passed each other 350 km away from Richmond Town. How far was Valley Town from Richmond Town?

18. A train, 100 m long, travels at a speed of 20 m/sec. How many seconds will it take to cross a bridge of 500 m long?

19. A train is 200 m long. How many seconds does it take for the train, traveling at 10 m/sec., to cross a bridge of 400 m long?

20. A train, 100 m long, takes 60 seconds to pass through a tunnel. If the tunnel is 380 m, how fast is the train traveling?

Singapore Math Challenge

The Age Problem

One of the most interesting mathematical topics is the computation of a person's age in relation to another's. Another problem of this nature is to find a person's age when it is a multiple of another person's age.

When attempting this type of problem, we should bear in mind that the difference between two ages will always remain unchanged. However, the multiple of one's age to another's age will change with time.

Below are the methods used to solve such problems.

1. Using a Model
2. Make a List
3. By Reasoning
4. Drawing

The first three methods are commonly used to solve problems of this nature. The last method, though not as commonly used, can help analyze the problems and solve them within a few working steps.

Example 1: The sum of the ages of two brothers is 28. The younger brother was 2 years younger than the older sibling ten years ago. How old are they now?

Method 1: Solve by Reasoning

The difference between two people's ages will always remain the same.

$28 \div 2 = 14$

$14 - 1 = 13$

$14 + 1 = 15$

Since their age difference is 2 years, the younger brother and his older sibling are 13 and 15 years old respectively.

Method 2: Solve Using a Model

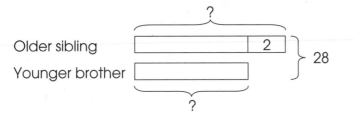

$28 - 2 = 26$

$26 \div 2 = 13$

The younger brother is 13 years old.

$13 + 2 = 15$

The older sibling is 15 years old.

Example 2: The sum of my parents' ages is 70. Twenty years ago, my father was 4 years older than my mother. How old are they now?

Method 1: Solve Using a Model

The difference of their ages is still 4 years.

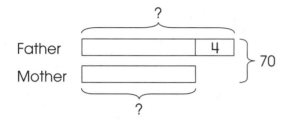

$70 - 4 = 66$

$66 \div 2 = 33$

My mother is 33 years old now.

$33 + 4 = 37$

My father is 37 years old now.

Method 2: Solve by Reasoning

$70 \div 2 = 35$

$35 - 2 = 33$

$35 + 2 = 37$

Since their age difference is 4 years, my mother and father are 33 and 37 years old now respectively.

Example 3: Sean is 26 years old. He is 8 years older than John. How many years ago was Sean's age three times John's age?

Method 1: Solve Using a Model

26 − 8 = 18
John is 18 years old now.

As the age difference is always the same,

8 ÷ 2 = 4

4 × 3 = 12

Sean was 12 years old when he was three times as old as John.

26 − 12 = 14

Sean's age was three times John's age 14 years ago.

Method 2: Make a List

Sean's age	John's age	Difference	Was Sean's age three times John's age?
26	18	8	No
24	16	8	No
20	12	8	No
16	8	8	No, 2 times only
14	6	8	No
12	4	8	Yes

26 − 12 = 14   or   18 − 4 = 14

Sean's age was three times John's age 14 years ago.

978-1-62399-074-9
Singapore Math Challenge

Example 4: Xavier is 2 years old and his mother is 26 years old. In how many years' time will his mother's age be three times Xavier's age?

Method 1: Solve Using a Model

26 – 2 = 24

Their age difference is 24 years.

24 ÷ 2 = 12

12 × 3 = 36

His mother will be 36 years old when she is three times older than Xavier.

36 – 26 = 10

His mother's age will be three times Xavier's age in 10 years' time.

Method 2: Make a List

Mother's age	Xavier's age	Difference	Was his mother's age three times Xavier's age?
26	2	24	No
30	6	24	No, 5 times
34	10	24	No
36	12	24	Yes

36 – 26 = 10   or   12 – 2 = 10

His mother's age will be three times Xavier's age in 10 years' time.

Example 5: The sum of John's age and his father's age is 44. Three years ago, the father was 20 years older than John. How old are they now?

Method 1: Solve by Reasoning

The difference between two people's ages will always remain the same.

$44 \div 2 = 22$

$22 - 10 = 12$

$22 + 10 = 32$

John and his father are now 12 and 32 years old respectively.

Method 2: Make a List

His father's age	John's age	Total	Does the difference equal 20?
36	8	44	No, it is 28.
34	10	44	No, it is 24.
32	12	44	Yes, it is 20.

John and his father are now 12 and 32 years old respectively.

978-1-62399-074-9
Singapore Math Challenge

Example 6: Raphael is 8 years old. One day, he asked his mother about her age. "When you reach my age, I will be 54 years old," replied his mother. How old is Raphael's mother?

Method 1: Solve by Drawing

The number of years it takes for Raphael to be as old as his mother is the same as the number of years it takes for his mother to be 54 years old.

$54 - 8 = 46$

$46 \div 2 = 23$

$23 + 8 = 31$

Raphael's mother is 31 years old.

1. Four years ago, the age of Isabelle's mother was 4 times Isabelle's age. Her mother is 44 years old. How old is Isabelle?

2. Joel is 8 years old. His mother is 34 years old. In how many years' time will his mother's age be three times Joel's age?

Method 1: Solve Using a Model

Method 2: Make a List

3. Beatrice is 10 years old. Her father is 34 years old. How many years ago was her father's age four times Beatrice's age?

Method 1: Solve Using a Model

Method 2: Make a List

4. The sum of Grandfather's age and Jimmy's age is 66. Three years later, Grandfather's age will be 8 times Jimmy's age. How old are Jimmy and his grandfather?

5. Samuel's grandmother is 64 years old. Samuel is 13 years old. In how many years' time will his grandmother's age be four times Samuel's age?

Solve Using a Model

6. The daughter is 8 years old. Her mother is 38 years old. In how many years' time will the mother's age be three times the daughter's age?

Method 1: Solve Using a Model

Method 2: Make a List

7. The sum of Melanie's and her brother's ages is 35. Four years from now, Melanie will be 5 years older than her brother. How old is Melanie? How old is her brother?

8. Jonathan is 10 years old. His brother, Joseph, is 14 years old. How old will each boy be when the sum of their ages is 50?

9. Granny Mabel is 60 years old. Kelly is 5 years old. In how many years' time will Granny Mabel's age be six times Kelly's age?

Method 1: Solve Using a Model

Method 2: Make a List

10. The father is 50 years old. His son is 24 years old. How many years ago was the father's age three times his son's age?

Method 1: Solve Using a Model

Method 2: Make a List

11. Jenevieve is 10 years old. She asks her teacher about her age. "I will be 58 years old by the time you reach my age," replies her teacher. How old is her teacher?

12. Cindy is 12 years old. She asks Auntie Zoe about her age. "I will be 62 years old by the time you reach my age," replies Auntie Zoe. How old is Auntie Zoe?

13. The sum of the father's and his son's ages is 60. The father's age was 3 times his son's age eight years ago. How old are they now?

14. The sum of the father's age and his daughter's age is 50. The father's age will be 3 times that of his daughter five years from now. How old is the father? How old is his daughter?

15. David's mother is 30 years older than him. Her age will be four times that of David eight years later. How old is David now?

16. Raymond's grandfather is 50 years older than him. His grandfather's age was six times that of Raymond six years ago. How old is Raymond's grandfather now?

Solve Using Models

The beauty of model drawing is its systematic approach and ease of application.

In the process of drawing models, the student will have a better understanding of the problem through its pictorial representation. In a well-drawn model, the student can almost get the correct answer instantly.

The examples illustrated in this chapter show how to use model drawing to solve problems involving sums, differences, multiples and fractions.

Example 1: Joe and Jason have $80 altogether. The amount of money Joe has is three times the amount of money Jason has. How much does Joe have?

Solution:

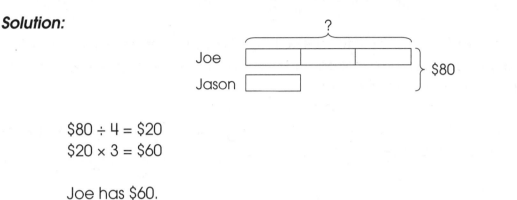

$80 ÷ 4 = $20
$20 × 3 = $60

Joe has $60.

Example 2: A farmer has 120 mares and stallions altogether. The number of mares is 20 more than the number of stallions. How many stallions does the farmer have?

Solution:

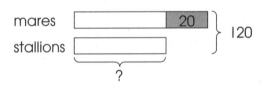

120 − 20 = 100
100 ÷ 2 = 50

The farmer has 50 stallions.

978-1-62399-074-9
Singapore Math Challenge

Example 3: There are 45 apples in carton A and 55 apples in carton B. How many apples must be transferred from carton B to carton A so that the number of apples in carton A is 3 times as many as the number of apples in carton B?

Solution:

carton A
carton B
} 45 + 55

$45 + 55 = 100$

There are a total of 100 apples in the two cartons.

$100 \div 4 = 25$

There are 25 apples in carton B in the end.

$25 \times 3 = 75$

There are 75 apples in carton A in the end.

$75 - 45 = 30$ or $55 - 25 = 30$

30 apples must be transferred from carton B to carton A.

Example 4: Alicia has $6 more than Betty. Betty has $10 more than Celia. The total amount of money they have is $116. How much money does each of them have?

Solution:

$116 - $10 - $10 - $6 = $90

$90 \div 3 = $30

Celia has $30.

$30 + $10 = $40

Betty has $40.

$40 + $6 = $46

Alicia has $46.

Alicia   ? $10 $6

Betty   ? $10

Celia   ?

} $116

Example 5: Alan, Benny and Charles have $240 in total. If Alan gives Benny $20 and Charles gives $15 to Benny, they will each have the same amount of money. How much money does each of them have at first?

Solution:

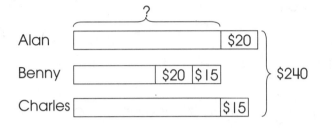

$240 ÷ 3 = $80
Each of them have $80 in the end.

$80 + $20 = $100
Alan has $100 at first.

$80 + $15 = $95
Charles has $95 at first.

$80 – $20 – $15 = $45
Benny has $45 at first.

Example 6: Millie had 180 trading cards at first. She gave $\frac{1}{9}$ of her cards to her best friend. She then gave $\frac{1}{4}$ of the remaining cards to her cousin. How many trading cards had she left?

Solution:

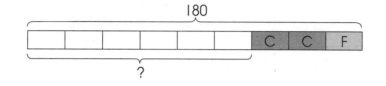

$\frac{1}{9} \times 180 = 20$

She gave 20 trading cards to her best friend.

$180 - 20 = 160$

$\frac{1}{4} \times 160 = 40$

She gave 40 trading cards to her cousin.

$160 - 40 = 120$
She had 120 trading cards left.

978-1-62399-074-9
Singapore Math Challenge

Example 7: Winnie and Patricia had an equal amount of money at first. After Winnie had spent $24 and Patricia had spent $72, Winnie had 3 times as much money as Patricia. How much money did each of them have at first?

Solution:

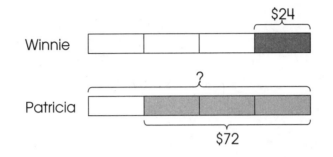

From the above model, each equal part is $24.

$24 × 4 = $96

Each of them had $96 at first.

978-1-62399-074-9
Singapore Math Challenge

Example 8: Mandy and Sue had the same number of beads at first. Mandy gave her cousin 19 beads. Sue's friend gave her 23 beads. Sue then had 3 times as many beads as Mandy. How many beads did each girl have at first?

Solution:

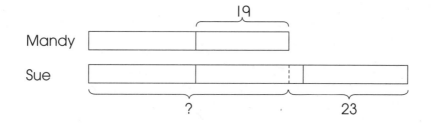

$19 + 23 = 42$

$42 \div 2 = 21$

Each equal part in the above model is 21.

$21 + 19 = 40$

OR

$(21 \times 3) - 23 = 40$

Each girl had 40 beads.

1. The reading corners in classes 3A and 3B have 152 books altogether. The number of books in the reading corner in class 3A is three times the number of books in the reading corner in class 3B. How many books are there in the reading corner in each class?

2. The sum of the ages of Jason and his younger brother is 15 years. If Jason's age is four times that of his brother, how old is his brother?

3. The sum of Valerie's and her father's ages is 50 years. If her father's age is four times that of Valerie, how old is Valerie?

4. There are 35 chickens and rabbits on a farm. The number of chickens is four times the number of rabbits. Find the number of chickens and the number of rabbits on the farm.

5. Peter and Paul received $300 altogether during the Chinese New Year. The amount of money Peter received was three times as much as the amount of money Paul received. How much money did each of them receive?

6. There are a total of 120 peach trees and apple trees in an orchard. The number of peach trees is 20 more than the number of apple trees. How many apple trees are there in the orchard?

7. John and Valerie plucked 60 peaches altogether during a farm visit in Australia. Valerie plucked 6 more than twice the number of peaches that John plucked. How many peaches did each of them pluck?

8. There are 200 goats on a farm altogether. The number of adult goats is 40 more than the number of kid goats. How many kid goats are on the farm?

978-1-62399-074-9
Singapore Math Challenge

9. Melvin has 45 storybooks and his brother has 75 storybooks. How many storybooks must Melvin give to his brother so that his brother has three times as many storybooks as Melvin?

10. Calvin has 30 colorful erasers. Jay has 45 such erasers. How many colorful erasers must Jay give Calvin so that the number of colorful erasers Calvin has is twice that of Jay?

11. There are 300 and 250 cows on Farms A and B respectively. How many cows from Farm A must be transferred to Farm B so that the number of cows on Farm B is four times the number of cows on Farm A?

12. The first rope is 7 m longer than the second rope. The second rope is 8 m longer than the third one. If the total length of these three ropes is 95 m, how long is each rope?

13. Alice has $5 more than Bryan. Bryan has $5 more than Cindy. Cindy has $5 more than Dylan. The total amount of money they have is $90. How much money does each of them have?

14. Container A contains 2 liters of water more than Container B. Container B contains 8 liters of water more than Container C. The total volume of these three containers is 54 liters. How many liters of water does each of the containers contain?

15. John, Sean and Andy save $1,160 altogether. John saves half of what Sean saves. Sean saves twice as much as Andy. How much money does each of them save?

16. 270 books are arranged on the 3 shelves of a bookcase. 20 books are taken from the first shelf and placed on the second shelf. 17 books are taken from the third shelf and placed on the second shelf. There is an equal number of books on the three shelves. How many books are on each shelf of the bookcase at first?

17. There are a total of 95 basketballs, footballs and volleyballs in the PE room. The number of volleyballs is twice the number of basketballs. The number of footballs is 5 fewer than the number of volleyballs. How many basketballs and how many volleyballs are there?

18. Michael's mother bought 1 liter of milk. Michael drank $\frac{1}{5}$ of the milk on the first day. Michael and his sister drank $\frac{1}{4}$ of the remaining milk on the second day. How much milk was left? (1 ℓ = 1,000 ml)

19. Janet ate $\frac{1}{6}$ of a family-sized pizza. His brother and sister ate $\frac{2}{5}$ of the remaining pizza. What fraction of the pizza was left?

20. Melanie's mother bought 1 liter of milk. Melanie poured $\frac{1}{4}$ of the milk into a big bowl of cereal in the morning. Her mother used $\frac{1}{3}$ of the remaining milk to make a cake in the afternoon. How much milk was left? ($1 \; \ell = 1,000$ ml)

21. There were the same number of cars in parking lots A and B at first. After 20 cars were driven out from parking lot A and 40 cars were driven out from parking lot B, the number of cars in parking lot A was twice the number of cars in parking lot B. How many cars were in parking lot A at first?

22. Two pieces of rope are the same length at first. When 6 m is cut from the first rope and 18 m is cut from the second rope, the length of the first rope is three times the length of the second rope. How long is each rope at first?

23. Vicky and Yvonne have the same amount of money at first. If Vicky spends $44 on a doll and Yvonne spends $11 on a present, the amount of money Yvonne has left is four times as much as Vicky. How much do they have altogether at first?

24. Natalie and Damien had the same number of marbles at first. Natalie gave 23 marbles to her friend. Damien's friend gave him 11 marbles. The number of marbles Damien had in the end was three times as many as the number of marbles Natalie had. How many marbles did each of them have at first?

25. Laura and Jolene had the same number of beads at first. Laura gave 29 beads to her friend. Jolene's friend gave her 33 beads. The number of beads Jolene had in the end was three times as many as the number of beads Laura had. How many beads did each of them have at first?

26. Jay and Jack had the same amount of money at first. Jay gave $35 to his brother. Jack's mother gave him another $25. The amount of money Jack had in the end was four times as much as the amount of money Jay had. How much money did each of them have at first?

Solve by Comparison and Replacement

First, the student must have a clear understanding of the problem. Next, break down the problem into more than one simpler problem. These simple problems can then be solved by two techniques, namely the **method of replacement** or **solve by comparison**.

The method of replacement is used when one item can be replaced by the other item when there is a link between both of them.

In the solve by comparison technique, we usually break down the problem into two mathematical statements. The next step is to bring the two mathematical statements to a comparable state by multiplication.

The examples in this chapter will show the application of the above-mentioned techniques.

Example 1: Two similar books and three identical pencil boxes cost $42. Two similar books and six identical pencil boxes cost $60. How much does each pencil box cost?

Analysis: Break down into 2 simple problems.

2 books + 3 pencil boxes → $42

2 books + 6 pencil boxes → $60

Since the number of books is the same, we can compare the pencil boxes.

6 pencil boxes − 3 pencil boxes → $60 − $42 = $18

3 pencil boxes → $18

1 pencil box   → $18 ÷ 3 = $6

Each pencil box cost $6.

Example 2: Four identical calculators and five similar staplers cost $78. Two such calculators and two such staplers cost $36. What is the cost of each stapler and each calculator?

Analysis: Break down into 2 simple problems.

4 calculators + 5 staplers → $78 ——— statement ①

2 calculators + 2 staplers → $36 ——— statement ②

To make statements 1 and 2 comparable, we multiply statement 2 by 2.

4 calculators + 4 staplers → $72

Use the technique — solve by comparison.

5 staplers – 4 staplers → $78 – $72

1 stapler → $6

4 calculators + (5 staplers × $6) → $78

4 calculators + $30 → $78

4 calculators → $78 – $30 = $48

1 calculator → $48 ÷ 4 = $12

The cost of each stapler is $6 and the cost of each calculator is $12.

Example 3: Two watermelons and three honeydews cost $48. The cost of each honeydew is twice as much as each watermelon. What is the cost of a watermelon?

    Analysis: 2 watermelons + 3 honeydews → $48 ——— statement ①

        Since each honeydew costs twice as much as each watermelon,

        1 honeydew = 2 watermelons

        So, 3 honeydews = 3 × 2
                         = 6 watermelons

        Replace 3 honeydews in statement 1 with 6 watermelons.

        2 watermelons + 6 watermelons → $48
                   8 watermelons → $48
                    1 watermelon → $48 ÷ 8 = $6

        The cost of a watermelon is $6.

Example 4: There are 78 students in classes 3A and 3B. There are 80 students in classes 3B and 3C. There are 82 students in classes 3A and 3C. How many students are there in each of the classes?

Analysis: Let the number of students in classes 3A, 3B and 3C be a, b and c respectively.

$a + b = 78$ equation ①

$b + c = 80$ equation ②

$a + c = 82$ equation ③

From the above three equations, we can conclude to the equation shown below.

$(2 \times a) + (2 \times b) + (2 \times c) = 78 + 80 + 82 = 240$

$a + b + c = 240 \div 2 = 120$

Since the total number of students in the three classes is 120, we can subtract each of the three equations from it to get the answers.

$c = 120 - 78 = 42$

$a = 120 - 80 = 40$

$b = 120 - 82 = 38$

There are 40, 38 and 42 students in classes 3A, 3B and 3C respectively.

1. 4 apples and 3 peaches cost $10.
4 apples and 6 peaches cost $16.
What is the cost of each peach?

2. 6 color ink cartridges and 3 black ink cartridges cost $150.
6 color ink cartridges and 5 black ink cartridges cost $170.
What is the cost of each color ink cartridge?

978-1-62399-074-9
Singapore Math Challenge

3. 3 similar chocolate bars and 4 similar packets of candy weigh 200 g.
3 such chocolate bars and 7 such packets of candy weigh 260 g. What is the weight
of a chocolate bar?

4. 3 similar boxes of apples and 5 similar boxes of oranges weigh 270 kg.
3 such boxes of apples and 7 such boxes of oranges weigh 342 kg.
How heavy are a box of apples and a box of oranges?

5. 4 identical jugs and 5 identical cups cost $85.
2 identical jugs and 2 identical cups cost $40.
What is the cost of a cup?

6. 4 apples and 3 peaches cost $10.
2 apples and 2 peaches cost $6.
What is the cost of an apple?

7. 5 identical basketballs and 6 identical volleyballs cost $320.
2 such basketballs and 3 such volleyballs cost $140.
What is the cost of a basketball?

8. 3 similar big pails and 4 similar small pails can hold 68 ℓ of water when they are filled to the brim. 4 such big pails and 2 such small pails can hold 64 ℓ of water. How much water can a big pail hold?

9. 1 table and 3 identical chairs cost $120. The table costs 3 times as much as each chair. What is the cost of the table?

10. 2 identical scooters and 3 identical bicycles cost $560. Each scooter costs twice as much as each bicycle. What is the cost of each scooter?

11. Mr. Cohen bought 4 identical tables and 9 identical chairs for $504. The cost of each table was the total cost for 3 such chairs. What was the cost of each chair?

12. Mr. Turner bought 4 identical basketballs and 5 identical volleyballs for $330. The price of 2 such basketballs was the same as the price of 3 such volleyballs. What was the price of a volleyball?

13. Mr. Saunders bought 4 similar basketballs and 5 similar volleyballs for $520. A few days later, he paid $533 for 5 such basketballs and 4 such volleyballs. How much were each basketball and each volleyball?

14. A basket contains some white, red and black balls. There are 15 white and red balls. There are 18 red and black balls. The number of black and white balls is 9. Find the number of balls for each color.

15. A florist sells some red, yellow and orange roses. She sells 60 red and yellow roses, 70 yellow and orange roses and 80 orange and red roses. Find the number of red roses, the number of yellow roses and the number of orange roses that the florist sells.

16. There are 87 adults and boys, 83 adults and girls and 60 boys and girls at a party. Find the number of adults, the number of boys and the number of girls at the party.

17. Melissa has 70 yellow and blue beads, 80 red and blue beads and 90 red and yellow beads. Find the number of beads of each different color that she has.

18. An sales assistant at a sports shop sells 100 blue and yellow flags, 90 red and blue flags and 80 yellow and red flags. Find the number of flags of each different color that he sells.

The Excess-and-Shortage Problem

Imagine you have some marbles. You are left with 6 marbles if you give each of your friends 11 marbles. You will need 12 more marbles if you give 14 marbles to each of your friends. How many friends do you give the marbles to? How many marbles do you have?

The above is an example of an excess-and-shortage problem. How do you solve problems of this nature when you are given two different scenarios? One of the scenarios illustrates an excess of items while the other illustrates a shortage of items.

In this chapter, the student will learn about the methods to solve such problems.

The following formulas are useful in solving problems of this nature.

Formula 1: (excess + shortage) ÷ difference = number of items

Formula 2: (excess – excess) ÷ difference = number of items

Formula 3: total = number of items × equal share for each item + excess

Formula 4: total = number of items × equal share for each item – shortage

Example 1: A teacher has a bag of candy. If she gives 10 pieces of candy to each of her students, there will be an excess of 8 pieces of candy. If she gives 11 pieces of candy to each of her students, she will need another 16 pieces of candy. How many students does the teacher give the pieces of candy to? How many pieces of candy does she have?

Solution:

excess pieces of candy = 8

shortage of pieces of candy = 16

difference in the number of pieces of candy = 11 − 10 = 1

Apply formula 1 to find the number of students.

(excess + shortage) ÷ difference = number of items

$$(8 + 16) \div 1 = 24$$

The teacher gives the pieces of candy to 24 students.

Apply formula 3 or 4 to find the number of pieces of candy.

total = number of items × equal share for each item + excess
= 24 × 10 + 8
= 248

OR

total = number of items × equal share for each item − shortage
= 24 × 11 − 16
= 248

She has 248 pieces of candy.

978-1-62399-074-9
Singapore Math Challenge

Example 2: A zookeeper gave bananas to a group of monkeys. If she gave 5 bananas to each monkey, she needed another 2 bananas. If she gave each monkey 4 bananas, there were 3 bananas left. How many monkeys were at the zoo? How many bananas did the zookeeper have?

Solution:

excess of bananas = 3

shortage of bananas = 2

difference in the number of bananas = 5 − 4 = 1

Apply formula 1 to find the number of monkeys.

(excess + shortage) ÷ difference = number of items

$$(3 + 2) ÷ 1 = 5$$

The zoo had 5 monkeys.

Apply formula 3 or 4 to find the number of bananas.

total = number of items × equal share for each item + excess
    = 5 × 4 + 3
    = 23

OR

total = number of items × equal share for each item − shortage
    = 5 × 5 − 2
    = 23

The zookeeper had 23 bananas.

978-1-62399-074-9
Singapore Math Challenge

Example 3: At a tree-planting project, each volunteer is supposed to plant the same number of trees. If each volunteer plants 5 trees, there will be 3 trees left. If each volunteer plants 3 trees, there will be 9 trees left. How many trees are planted? How many volunteers are there?

Solution:

excess of trees = 3

excess of trees = 9

difference in the number of trees = 5 – 3 = 2

Apply formula 2 to find the number of volunteers.

(excess – excess) ÷ difference = number of items

$$(9 - 3) ÷ 2 = 3$$

There are 3 volunteers.

Apply formula 3 to find the number of trees.

total = number of items × equal share for each item + excess

= 3 × 5 + 3

= 18

OR

= 3 × 3 + 9 = 18

18 trees are planted.

1. A teacher has a bag of candy. If she gives each pupil 8 pieces of candy, she will be left with 8 pieces of candy. If she gives each pupil 10 pieces of candy, she needs 4 more pieces of candy. How many pupils does the teacher give the pieces of candy to? How many pieces of candy does she have?

2. A carton of oranges is to be shared among some family members. If each family member gets 5 oranges, there will be 3 oranges left in the carton. If every family member gets 7 oranges, there is a shortage of 7 oranges. How many members are there in this family? How many oranges are there in this carton?

3. Mr. Nelson is changing the water in his fish tank. If he uses a 5-liter pail, 4 liters of water will overflow. If he uses a 3-liter pail, he needs another 4 more pails of water. How many liters of water are needed to fill the fish tank?

4. Greenville Primary School is organizing a field trip for the students. If the seating capacity of each bus is 35 students, 5 students will not be able to board the bus. If the seating capacity of each bus is 40 students, there will be an extra empty bus. How many buses are needed for the field trip? How many students are going on the field trip?

978-1-62399-074-9
Singapore Math Challenge

5. A comic costs $3 and a mystery book costs $5 each. If Ken spends all his money on the comics, he has $6 left. If he wants to buy all mystery books, he needs another $8. How many comics or mystery books is Ken buying? How much money does he have?

6. A teacher is taking some students for a riverboat excursion. If each boat can take only 3 students, 16 students will not get onto the boat. If each boat can take only 5 students, 2 students will not get onto the boat. How many boats are there? How many students are there?

7. Mrs. Bunny was giving away some carrots to her children. If each rabbit received 3 carrots, there would be an excess of 7 carrots. If each rabbit was given 4 carrots, there would be only 2 carrots left. How many children did Mrs. Bunny give the carrots to? How many carrots did she have?

8. If 6 students are sharing a hostel room in an international school, there will be 2 empty rooms. If 4 students are sharing a hostel room instead, there will be a shortage of 3 rooms. How many students want to stay in the hostel? How many hostel rooms does the international school have?

978-1-62399-074-9
Singapore Math Challenge

9. Miss Atkinson stayed after school to grade some papers. If she graded 4 questions in a minute, she would leave the school 5 minutes late. If she graded 6 questions in a minute, she would leave the school 5 minutes early. How many questions did she grade before she left the school?

10. Jodi walks to school every morning. If she walks at a speed of 50 meters per minute, she will be 4 minutes late for school. If she walks at a speed of 65 meters per minute, she will reach her school 2 minutes before the bell rings. How long does Jodi take to walk to school in order to be on time? How far is the school from her house?

Finding Cubes

1. How many cubes are there in each of the figures shown below?

(a)

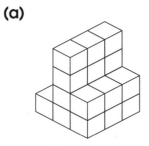

(b)

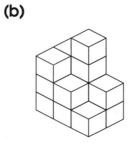

(c)

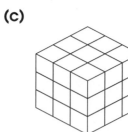

(d)

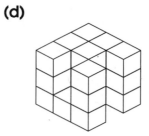

2. How many cubes are there in each of the figures shown below?

(a)

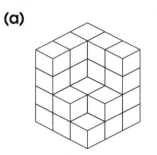

(b)

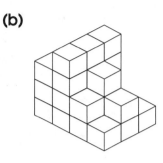

(c)

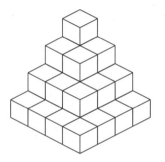

(d) The darkened part is hollow.

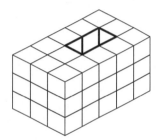

3. How many cubes are there in each of the figures shown below?

(a) The darkened part is hollow.

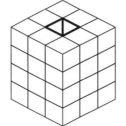

(b)

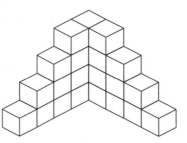

(c)

4. 27 identical cubes are used to form the cuboid shown below. Six faces of the cuboid are then painted in yellow. Complete the table below to show the number of cubes with different numbers of faces painted yellow.

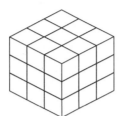

No. of faces painted yellow	0	1	2	3	4	5	6	
No. of cubes								Total:

5. The I-shaped object below is made up of 9 identical cubes. The surface of the object is painted blue. After the paint dries, the cubes are separated. Complete the table below to show the number of cubes with different numbers of faces painted blue.

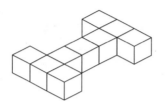

No. of faces painted blue	0	1	2	3	4	5	6	
No. of cubes								Total:

6. The figure shown below is made up of 12 identical cubes. It is then painted green before all the cubes are separated. Complete the table below to show the number of cubes with different numbers of faces painted green.

No. of faces painted green	0	1	2	3	4	5	6	
No. of cubes								Total:

IQ Problems

There are no fixed methods for solving problems of this nature.

The first step is to read and understand the problem. Next, devise a plan that might be able to solve the problem. Lastly, try to solve the problem with the plan.

Sometimes, it takes more than one attempt to solve the problem.

If your first plan does not work, devise another plan.

Keep trying until you succeed. It is important to persevere in the learning of mathematics.

Example 1: The map of a city is shown below. Vehicles can travel on the roads between the buildings indicated by gray boxes below. In how many ways can a car travel from Point A to Point B? (Assume that the car does not go backward.)

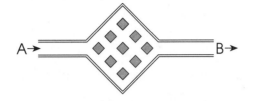

Solution:

The numbers indicate the number of ways the car can travel to different junctions.

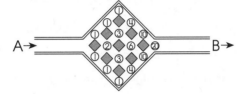

Step 1:   The car can start driving from any points marked 1.

Step 2:   1 + 1 = 2 ways

Step 3:   1 + 2 = 3 ways

Step 4:   1 + 3 = 4 ways
           3 + 3 = 6 ways

Step 5:   6 + 4 = 10 ways
           10 + 10 = 20 ways

A car can travel from Point A to Point B in 20 ways.

Example 2: Many years ago, there were 4 Mondays and 4 Fridays in the month of March. On which day was March 1st in that year?

Solution:

There are 31 days in the month of March.

$31 \div 7 = 4 \text{ R } 3$

This means that 4 days of the week happened 4 times in that month and 3 days of the week happened 5 times.

Clearly, the first day could not be on Friday, Saturday, Sunday or Monday, otherwise there would be 5 Fridays or 5 Saturdays and so on.

Another way to reason is the extra 3 days could only fit in between Monday and Friday.

So, the first day of that month was a Tuesday.

We can confirm the answer by using the table shown below.

Sun.	Mon.	Tues.	Wed.	Thurs.	Fri.	Sat.
		1	2	3	4	5
6	7	8	9	10	11	12
13	14	15	16	17	18	19
20	21	22	23	24	25	26
27	28	29	30	31		

March 1st in that year was on Tuesday.

Example 3: There are 3 red socks, 3 blue socks, 3 yellow socks and 3 gray socks in a drawer. If Betty is blindfolded, how many socks must she take from the drawer one at a time so that at least two of the socks are of the same color?

Solution:

Though it is possible to get two socks of the same color after two draws, we always consider the worst-case scenario in problems of this nature.

Red	Blue	Yellow	Gray
I	I	I	I

As shown above, we could have drawn one sock of each color before we are able to make a pair of same colored socks.

Therefore, she must take 5 socks from the drawer so that at least two of the socks are of the same color.

978-1-62399-074-9
Singapore Math Challenge

1. In how many ways can you form the word "WATER" from the network shown below?

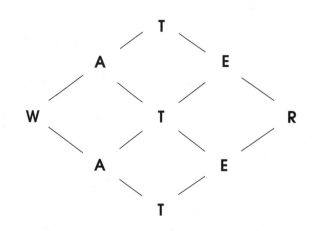

2. Many years ago, there were 4 Thursdays and 4 Mondays in the month of January. On which day was January 1st in that year? (Use the table to confirm your answer.)

Sun.	Mon.	Tue.	Wed.	Thu.	Fri.	Sat.

3. There are 15 gold coins. One of the gold coins is a fake. A fake gold coin is lighter than a real one. You have a "balance machine" without any scale. Can you identify the fake coin by using the "balance machine" at most three times?

4. There is one 40-ml cup and one 70-ml cup. Lily needs just 20 ml of water. Are you able to help her using just the two cups?

5. The area of a lily pond covered by leaves doubled every day. If the pond was covered with leaves on the 16th day, on which day was the pond half-covered with leaves?

6. Many years ago, there were 4 Thursdays and 4 Mondays in the month of March. On which day was March 10th in that year? (Use the table below to confirm your answer.)

Sun.	Mon.	Tue.	Wed.	Thu.	Fri.	Sat.

7. An ant is about to travel from Point A to Point B using the edges of the cube shown below. In how many ways can the ant travel?

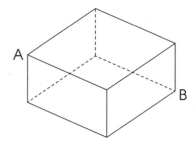

8. Mrs. Rabbit had 28 carrots to give away to her 7 good friends. If each friend received a different number of carrots, how many carrots would each of them get?

9. Divide each square below into 4 identical shapes. Show at least 5 different ways to obtain 4 identical shapes.

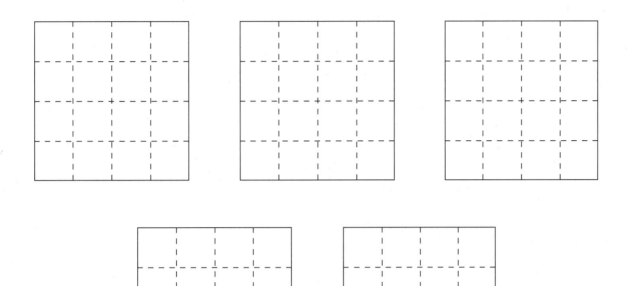

10. The yellow, red, blue and green lights are able to make many types of signals. These signals can be made from one light, two lights, three lights or four lights at the same time. How many different signals can these lights make?

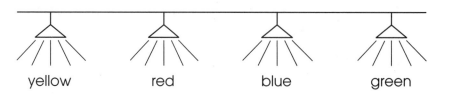

yellow   red   blue   green

11. There are six train stations between City A and City B. Commuters can buy tickets to each train station at any of the six train stations. How many types of train tickets can be purchased between City A and City B?

City A   City B

12. There is one handshake between every two people. How many handshakes are there among 6 people?

13. How many ways can an ant go from Point A to Point B if it can only move along the direction indicated by the arrows?

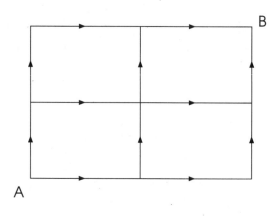

14. An ant is trying to crawl from Point A to Point B by the shortest route. This means that only upward and left-to-right movements are allowed. A spider is waiting at Point C. In how many ways can the ant crawl from Point A to Point B without going through Point C?

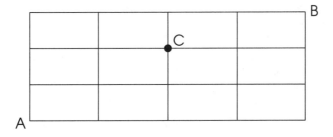

15. Cindy originally planned to read her storybook at the rate of 12 pages a day. She ended up reading 8 pages more every day and finished reading the storybook 2 days in advance. How many pages were in the storybook?

16. How many ways can you form the word "FLOWERS" from the network shown below?

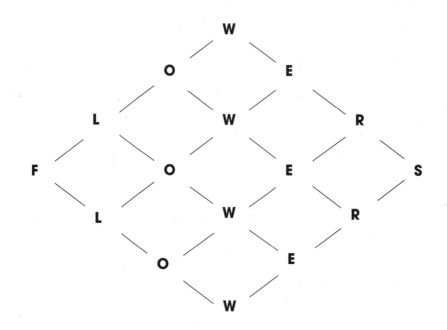

17. 30 students numbered from 1 to 30 were asked to line up in a straight line. The first student in the line was asked to leave, the second student remained. The third student was asked to leave the line, the fourth student remained and so forth. This process was then repeated until there was only one student left in the line. What was the number of the only student?

18. A droplet of oil drops onto the surface of a bowl of water. The surface that the oil covers is twice the surface that it covered a minute ago. If it takes 4 minutes to cover the whole surface of the bowl of water, when does the oil cover $\frac{1}{4}$ of the surface of a bowl of water?

19. There are 8 cards. Each card is numbered consecutively from 1 to 8. The sum of the numbers on the two cards Alice has drawn is 13. The sum of the numbers on the two cards Beatrice has drawn is 11. The sum of the numbers on the two cards Cindy has drawn is 8. Which two cards will Diana draw?

20. At a certain stage of growth, a worm grew twice as long as it was the day before. If the worm measured 40 mm on the 14th day, how many days did it take to grow to 5 mm long?

Interesting Remainder Problems

We will learn about dividends, divisors, quotients and remainders in this chapter.

There are many interesting mathematical problems related to division. First, let us find out more about the technical names in division.

$$17 \div 3 = 5 \, R \, 2$$

17 is the dividend,

3 is the divisor,

5 is the quotient,

2 is the remainder.

Example 1: Fill in each blank with the correct number so that the remainder is the largest.

$$\boxed{} \div 4 = 7\ \text{R}\ \boxed{}$$

Solution:

The largest remainder must be smaller than the divisor.

So, we have

$$\boxed{} \div 4 = 7\ \text{R}\ 3$$

working backward

$$4 \times 7 + 3 = 31$$

$$\boxed{31} \div 4 = 7\ \text{R}\ \boxed{3}$$

Example 2: Fill in each blank with the correct number so that the divisor is the smallest.

$$\boxed{} \div \boxed{} = 5\ \text{R}\ 3$$

Solution:

The divisor is the smallest when it is 1 more than the remainder.

So, we have

$$\boxed{} \div 4 = 5\ \text{R}\ 3$$

working backward

$$4 \times 5 + 3 = 23$$

$$\boxed{23} \div \boxed{4} = 5\ \text{R}\ 3$$

Example 3: Beads are strung on a string in a pattern of two white beads then three black beads as shown below.

What is the color of the 37th bead?
What is the color of the 49th bead?

Solution:

We need only to consider a block of 5 beads since its pattern repeats after every 5 beads.

○	○	●	●	●
R1	R2	R3	R4	0

$37 \div 5 = 7 \text{ R } 2$

The color of the 37th bead is white.

$49 \div 5 = 9 \text{ R } 4$

The color of the 49th bead is black.

Example 4: Many years ago, the first day in the month of January was a Sunday. On which day of the week was January 25th in that year?

Solution:

There are 7 days in a week.

$25 \div 7 = 3 \text{ R } 4$

Sun.	Mon.	Tue.	Wed.	Thurs.	Fri.	Sat.
R1	R2	R3	R4	R5	R6	0

Therefore, January 25th in that year was Wednesday.

Example 5: 1   2   3   4   1   2   3   4   1   2   3   4   ...

> What is the 35th number?
>
> What is the sum of the first 36 numbers?

Solution:

The numbers repeat themselves after every four numbers.

$$35 \div 4 = 8 \text{ R } 3$$

1	2	3	4
R1	R2	R3	0

The 35th number is 3.

$$1 + 2 + 3 + 4 = 10$$

$$36 \div 4 = 9 \text{ blocks of } 10$$

$$9 \times 10 = 90$$

The sum of the first 36 numbers is 90.

1. Fill in each box with the correct answer so that the divisor is the smallest.

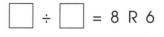

$$\boxed{} \div \boxed{} = 8 \text{ R } 6$$

2. Fill in each box with the correct answer so that the remainder is the largest.

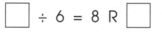

$$\boxed{} \div 6 = 8 \text{ R } \boxed{}$$

3. Find the missing numbers.

$$37 \div \boxed{} = \boxed{} \text{ R } 7$$

4. What are the possible dividends when the quotient and the remainder are the same? (There are 5 answers.)

$$\boxed{} \div 6 = \boxed{} \text{ R } \boxed{}$$

5. A string of black and white beads are arranged in the way shown below.

⬤ ⬤ ⬤ ○ ○ ⬤ ⬤ ⬤ ○ ○ ⬤ ⬤ ⬤ ○ ○ ...

What is the color of the 24ᵗʰ bead?

What is the color of the 198ᵗʰ bead?

6. ○ ○ △ △ △ □ ○ ○ △ △ △ □ ○ ○ △ △ △ □ ...

What is the shape of the 38ᵗʰ figure?

What is the shape of the 59ᵗʰ figure?

978-1-62399-074-9
Singapore Math Challenge

7. The numbers 2, 3 and 4 are repeated in a pattern as shown below.

3 2 4 3 2 4 3 2 4 ...

What is the digit of the 28th number in the pattern?
What is the sum of the first 33 numbers?

8. The numbers 3, 4, 5 and 6 are written in the pattern below.

3 6 4 5 3 6 4 5 3 6 4 5 ...

What is the digit of the 35th number?
What is the sum of the first 18 numbers?

978-1-62399-074-9
Singapore Math Challenge

9. Many years ago, the 1st of July was on Monday. On which day of the week was the 25th of July in that year?

10. Many years ago, the 10th of March was on Tuesday. On which day of the week was the 11th of May in that year?

11. 48 playing cards are distributed among five children in this manner.

Jessica	Melissa	Natalie	Alison	Kelly
1	2	3	4	5
6	7	8	9	10
11	12	…	…	…

Who will get the last card?

12. 36 playing cards are distributed among four children in this manner.

Carson	Joan	Chloe	Amanda
1	2	3	4
8	7	6	5
9	10	…	…

Who will get the last card?

13. Many years ago, the 10ᵗʰ of March was on Monday. Which day of the week would it be 30 days later?

14. 200 playing cards are given away to a group of children in this manner.

Alice	Ben	Chloe	Dylon	Elaine	Florence
1	2	3	4	5	6
7	8	9	10	11	12
...	...	...	...	...	...

Who will get the 150ᵗʰ card?
Who will get the last card?

15. When 149 is divided by a 2-digit number, it has a remainder of 5. Find all the 2-digit divisors.

16. A number has a remainder of 2 when it is divided by 3. It has a remainder of 3 when it is divided by 4. Find two such numbers that are smaller than 30.

978-1-62399-074-9
Singapore Math Challenge

17. A number has a remainder of 2 when it is divided by 3. It has a remainder of 3 when it is divided by 5. The remainder is again 2 when the divisor is 7. Find the number.

18. In a division statement, the quotient is 9 and its remainder is 2. The sum of the dividend and the divisor is 42. Find the values of the dividend and the divisor.

19. In a division statement, the quotient is 5 and its remainder is 6. The difference between the divisor and the dividend is 38. Find the values of the dividend and the divisor.

20. If Mary reads 90 pages a day, it will take her more than 4 days to finish reading a storybook. If she reads 80 pages a day, she will take less than 5 days. If the number of days Mary takes to finish reading is the same as the number of pages she reads every day, how many pages must she read every day?

Finding Perimeter

The formula to find the perimeter of a square is known as

side + side + side + side   **or**

4 × side

The formula to find the perimeter of a rectangle is known as

width + width + length + length   **or**

2 × width + 2 × length

The technique shown in this chapter involves "changing" a figure to a square or a rectangle whenever possible so as to make the computation simpler.

978-1-62399-074-9
Singapore Math Challenge

Example 1: Find the perimeter of the following figures.

(a)

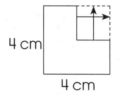

4 cm

4 cm

(b)

3 cm

6 cm

Solution:

(a) If we "push" the two lines as shown, the figure becomes a square.

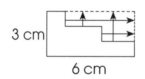

4 cm

4 cm

Perimeter = 4 × 4 cm
= 16 cm

(b) Likewise, if we push the four lines as shown, the figure becomes a rectangle.

3 cm

6 cm

Perimeter = 3 cm × 2 + 6 cm × 2
= 6 cm + 12 cm
= 18 cm

Example 2: The figure below is made up of 6 identical squares. If the figure has a perimeter of 28 cm, what is the length of each side of a square?

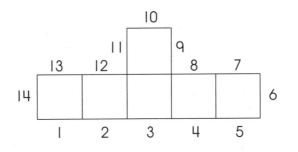

Solution:

There are 14 sides altogether.

$$28 \div 14 = 2 \text{ cm}$$

The length of each side of a square is 2 cm.

978-1-62399-074-9
Singapore Math Challenge

I. Find the perimeter of the following figures.

(a)

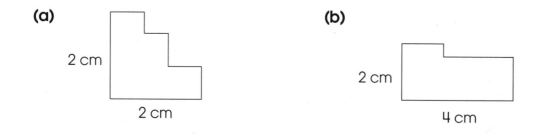

2 cm

2 cm

(b)

2 cm

4 cm

(c)

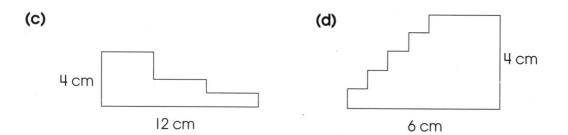

4 cm

12 cm

(d)

4 cm

6 cm

978-1-62399-074-9
Singapore Math Challenge

2. Find the perimeter of the following figures.

(a)

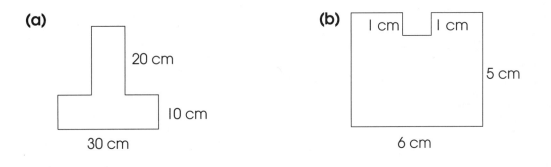

20 cm

10 cm

30 cm

(b)

I cm   I cm

5 cm

6 cm

(c)

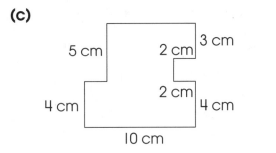

5 cm   2 cm   3 cm

4 cm   2 cm   4 cm

10 cm

(d)

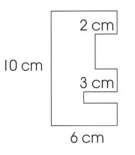

2 cm

10 cm

3 cm

6 cm

978-1-62399-074-9
Singapore Math Challenge

3. An ant is crawling from Point A to Point B using the staircase. How many meters will it crawl to reach Point B?

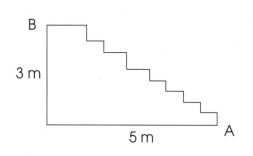

4. The figure shown below is made up of 5 identical squares.
If the perimeter of the figure is 36 cm, what is the length of each side of a square?

5. In the figure below, the original rectangle was cut into 6 smaller identical rectangles. What is the perimeter of each small rectangle?

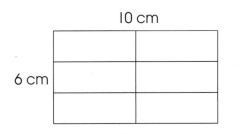

6. The figure below is made up of identical squares with sides that are 6 cm in length. What is its perimeter?

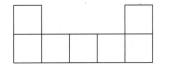

7. A wire with a length of 84 cm is used to form a square with sides that are 8 cm in length. The remaining wire is then used to form a rectangle with a width of 10 cm. What is the length of the rectangle?

8. The figure below is made up of two squares, A and B. The perimeter of square A is 28 cm. What is the perimeter of the figure?

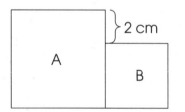

9. A wire with a length of 150 cm is used to form a square with sides that are 15 cm in length. The remaining wire is used to form a rectangle with a length of 25 cm. What is the width of the rectangle?

10. Find the perimeter of the figure which is made up of 7 identical rectangles with a length of 15 cm.

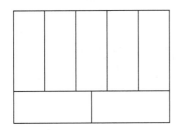

11. The perimeter of a rectangle is 2 times that of a square. The width of the rectangle and the side of the square are both 15 cm. What is the length of the rectangle?

12. The square shown below is made of 4 identical rectangles. The perimeter of each rectangle is 20 cm. What is the perimeter of the square?

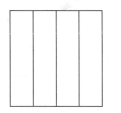

978-1-62399-074-9
Singapore Math Challenge

13. Figures A and B are made up of identical squares. If the perimeter of Figure A is 25 cm, what is the perimeter of Figure B?

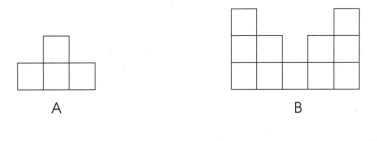

A   B

14. A rectangle and a square have the same perimeter. The side of the square is 14 cm. The length of the rectangle is 3 times its width. What are the length and width of the rectangle?

The Page-Number Problem

When you first get a storybook, what do you normally do?

Some readers like to read the features at the back of the book, some like to scan through the table of contents and others will read the introduction for a better idea of the storybook. Most readers certainly will be interested to know the number of pages of the storybook.

So, we will learn more about problems related to page numbers.

In this chapter, we will learn

(a)   how to find the total digits used in the printing of the page numbers of a book,

(b)   how to find the thickness of a book based on the given total number of digits.

978-1-62399-074-9
Singapore Math Challenge

Example 1: Sharon bought a 140-page book. How many digits have been used for the page numbers in the book?

Solution:

Page 1 to Page 9 : 9 digits

Page 10 to Page 99 : 99 – 10 = 89

89 + 1 = 90 page numbers

90 × 2 = 180 digits

Page 100 to Page 140 : 140 – 100 = 40

40 + 1 = 41 page numbers

41 × 3 = 123 digits

9 + 180 + 123 = 312

312 digits have been used for the page numbers in the book.

Example 2: How many digits are used for the page numbers in a book that has 325 pages?

Solution:

Page 1 to Page 9   : 9 digits

Page 10 to Page 99   : 99 – 10 = 89

89 + 1 = 90 page numbers

90 × 2 = 180 digits

Page 100 to Page 325 : 325 – 100 = 225

225 + 1 = 226 page numbers

226 × 3 = 678 digits

9 + 180 + 678 = 867

867 digits are used for the page numbers in a book that has 325 pages.

Example 3: A book uses 519 digits altogether for its page numbers. How many pages does the book have?

Solution:

Page 1 to Page 9   : 9 digits

Page 10 to Page 99 : 180 digits

519 – 9 – 180 = 330 digits

The remaining pages use 330 digits.

330 digits belong to the 3-digit numbers, starting from Page 100.

330 ÷ 3 = 110

99 + 110 = 209

The book has 209 pages.

978-1-62399-074-9
Singapore Math Challenge

Example 4: A book uses 1,152 digits for printing its page numbers. How many pages has the book?

Solution:

Page 1 to Page 9   : 9 digits

Page 10 to Page 99 : 180 digits

1,152 − 9 − 180 = 963 digits

The remaining pages use 963 digits.

963 digits belong to the 3-digit numbers, starting from Page 100.

963 ÷ 3 = 321

99 + 321 = 420

The book has 420 pages.

1. How many digits are used for printing the page numbers of a book that has 185 pages?

2. How many digits are there from numbers 1 to 200?

3. How many digits are in a book that has 345 pages?

4. How many digits are there from numbers 1 to 500?

5. A book uses 648 digits for printing its page numbers. How many pages does the book have?

6. A book uses 792 digits for printing its page numbers. How many pages does the book have?

7. A storybook uses 1,014 digits for its page numbers. How thick is the storybook?

8. A book uses 1,248 digits for printing its page numbers. How thick is the book?

Counting

In this chapter, we will learn to count systematically so as not to miss or repeat any count. To achieve this aim, we keep a record of what has already been counted using symbols in order to avoid confusion.

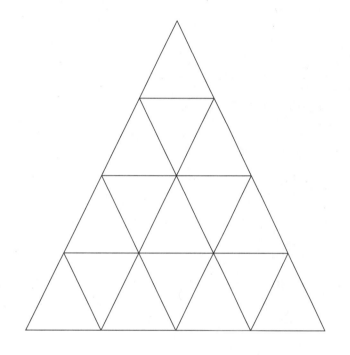

Example 1: How many triangles are there in the figures shown below?

(a)

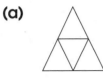

(b)

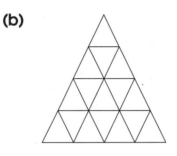

Solution:

(a)   Number of triangles formed by 1 △   = 4

Number of triangles formed by 4 △s = 1

Total number of △s = 1 + 4 = 5

(b)   Number of triangles formed by 1 △   = 16

Number of triangles formed by 4 △s = 7

Number of triangles formed by 9 △s = 3

Number of triangles formed by 16 △s = 1

Total number of △s = 16 + 7 + 3 + 1 = 27

Example 2: How many squares are there in the figures shown below?

(a)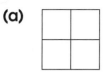

(b)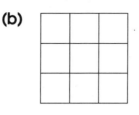

Solution:

(a) Number of squares formed by 1 □ = 4

Number of squares formed by 4 □s = 1

Total number of □s = 4 + 1 = 5

(b) Number of squares formed by 1 □ = 9

Number of squares formed by 4 □s = 4

Number of squares formed by 9 □s = 1

Total number of □s = 9 + 4 + 1 = 14

1. How many triangles are there in each of the following figures?

(a)

(b)

2. How many squares are there in each of the following figures?

(a)

(b)

3. Count the number of triangles in each of the following figures.

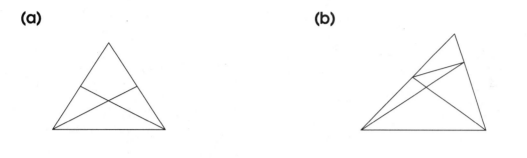

(a)

(b)

4. Count the number of rectangles in parts **(a)** and **(b)**.

(a)

(b)

5. Count the number of triangles in parts **(a)** and **(b)**.

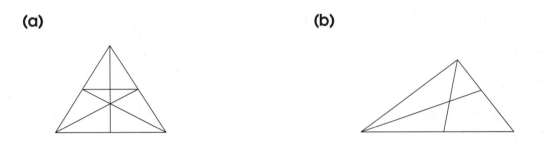

(a)   **(b)**

6. How many rectangles are there in the figure shown below?

7. How many triangles are there in the figures shown below?

(a)

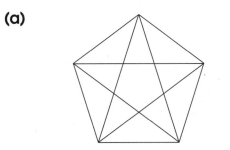

(b)

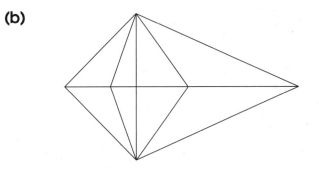

Solutions

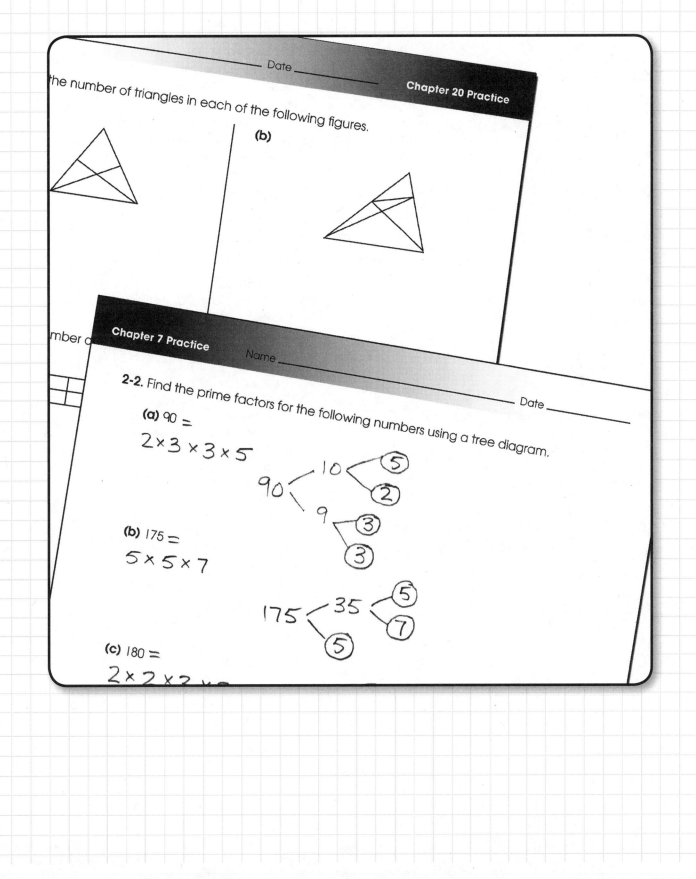

Chapter 20 Practice

the number of triangles in each of the following figures.

(b)

mber o

2-2. Find the prime factors for the following numbers using a tree diagram.

— Date _____

(a) 90 =

$2 \times 3 \times 3 \times 5$

90 ⟨ 10 ⟨ 5
         2
     9 ⟨ 3
         3

(b) 175 =

$5 \times 5 \times 7$

175 ⟨ 35 ⟨ 5
          7
      5

(c) 180 =

$2 \times 2 \times 2 \times$

Chapter 1 Practice

Page 10

1. **(a)** This is an example of Fibonacci numbers.

    $1 + 1 = 2$,
    $1 + 2 = 3$,
    $2 + 3 = 5$,
    $3 + 5 = 8$,
    $5 + 8 = 13$.

    (b) The fifth term is the sum of the first four terms. In essence, each term is the sum of the preceding four terms.

    $1 + 1 + 1 + 1 = 4$,
    $1 + 1 + 1 + 4 = 7$,
    $1 + 1 + 4 + 7 = 13$,
    $1 + 4 + 7 + 13 = 25$.

    (c) The difference between two terms increases by 2 each time.

    $3 + 2 = 5$,
    $5 + 4 = 9$,
    $9 + 6 = 15$,
    ... ,
    $45 + 14 = 59$.

    (d) The difference between two terms increases by 1 each time.

    $1 + 2 = 3$,
    $3 + 3 = 6$,
    $6 + 4 = 10$,
    ... ,
    $10 + 5 = 15$.

    (e) The difference between two terms is growing consecutive odd numbers.

    $0 + 3 = 3$,
    $3 + 5 = 8$,
    $8 + 7 = 15$,
    ... ,
    $24 + 11 = 35$.

    (f) Each term is multiplied by consecutive numbers, starting from 2.

    $1 \times 2 = 2$,
    $2 \times 3 = 6$,
    $6 \times 4 = 24$,
    $24 \times 5 = 120$,
    $120 \times 6 = 720$.

    (g) The sum of the first and third terms is equal to the multiplication of the second term and 3. This rule applies to all terms in the number pattern.

    $0 + 3 = 1 \times 3$,
    $1 + 8 = 3 \times 3$,
    $3 + 21 = 8 \times 3$,
    $8 + 55 = 21 \times 3$,
    $21 + (\quad) = 55 \times 3$,
    therefore $(\quad) = 165 - 21 = 144$,
    $55 + (\quad) = 144 \times 3$,
    therefore $(\quad) = 432 - 55 = 377$.

    (h) Each term is increased by twice the previous increment.

    $1 + ②= 3$,
    $3 + ④= 7$,
    $7 + ⑧= 15$,
    $15 + ⑯= 31$,
    $31 + ㉜= 63$,
    $63 + ㉞= 127$.

    (i) The rule below is applicable to all terms except for the first one.

    Rule: previous term + 2 × (order of the term − 2)

    $1 + 2 \times (3rd - 2) = 3$,
    $3 + 2 \times (4th - 2) = 7$,
    $7 + 2 \times (5th - 2) = 13$,
    $13 + 2 \times (6th - 2) = 13 + 8 = 21$.

    (j) The rule is the same as the one stated in part (g).

    $1 + 5 = 2 \times 3$,
    $2 + 13 = 5 \times 3$,
    $5 + 34 = 13 \times 3$,
    $13 + 89 = 34 \times 3$,
    $34 + (\quad) = 89 \times 3$
    therefore $(\quad) = 267 - 34 = 233$.
    $89 + (\quad) = 233 \times 3$
    therefore $(\quad) = 699 - 89 = 610$.

Page 11

2. Rule 1: The answers always end with 89.
Rule 2: The first digit increases with each answer.
Rule 3: The first digit indicates the number of 8s in the answers.
$54,321 \times 9 = 488,889$
$654,321 \times 9 = 5,888,889$
$7,654,321 \times 9 = 68,888,889$
$87,654,321 \times 9 = 788,888,889$
$987,654,321 \times 9 = 8,888,888,889$

3. Rule: Each answer is the sum of the two numbers directly above it.
1 (5) (10) (10) (5) 1
1 (6) (15) (20) (15) (6) 1
1 (7) (21) (35) (35) (21) (7) 1

Page 12

4. $101 \times 44 = 4,444$
$101 \times 55 = 5,555$
$101 \times 66 = 6,666$
$101 \times 77 = 7,777$
$101 \times 88 = 8,888$
$101 \times 99 = 9,999$

Page 13

5. **(a)** $30 - 10 = 20$, $20 \times 2 = 40$.
$24 - 10 = 14$, $14 \times 2 = 28$.
$25 - 10 = 15$, $15 \times 2 = 30$.
(b) $14 + 8 = 22$, $22 \div 2 = 11$.
$12 + 8 = 20$, $20 \div 2 = 10$.
$20 + 8 = 28$, $28 \div 2 = 14$.
(c) $18 + 5 = 23$, $23 - 8 = 15$.
$14 + 5 = 19$, $19 - 8 = 11$.
$17 + 5 = 22$, $22 - 8 = 14$.
(d) $8 \times 6 = 48$, $48 - 16 = 32$.
$9 \times 6 = 54$, $54 - 16 = 38$.
$7 \times 6 = 42$, $42 - 16 = 26$.
(e) $3 \times 4 = 12$, $12 + 12 = 24$.
$8 \times 4 = 32$, $32 + 12 = 44$.
$20 \times 4 = 80$, $80 + 12 = 92$.

Page 14

6. In this number pattern, we have to use the "guess-and-check" method.
$18 + 12 = 30$
$29 + 12 = 41$
$5 + 12 = 17$
$12 + 12 = 24$
$44 + 12 = 56$
All the digits from 1 to 9 are used.

7. The method is the same as the one stated in question 6.
$8 \times 4 + 5 = 37$
$16 \times 4 + 5 = 69$
$5 \times 4 + 5 = 25$
$23 \times 4 + 5 = 97$
$14 \times 4 + 5 = 61$
All the digits from 1 to 9 are used.

8. The method is the same as the one stated in question 6.
$8 \div 2 - 1 = 3$
$12 \div 2 - 1 = 5$
$30 \div 2 - 1 = 14$
$46 \div 2 - 1 = 22$
$96 \div 2 - 1 = 47$
All the digits from 1 to 9 are used.

Page 15

9. The method is the same as the one stated in question 6.

$16 \times 2 + 3 = 35$
$14 \times 2 + 3 = 31$
$15 \times 2 + 3 = 33$
$27 \times 2 + 3 = 57$
$18 \times 2 + 3 = 39$

All the digits from 1 to 9 are used.

10. There are more than one set of answers to this question. The key is to put an equal number of balls in each corner.

Ans 1 $32 - 4 = 28$
$28 \div 4 = 7$
If there are 7 balls in each of the four corners, each of the remaining boxes contains 1 ball.

Ans 2 $32 - 8 = 24$
$24 \div 4 = 6$
If there are 6 balls in each of the four corners, each of the remaining boxes contains 2 balls.

Ans 3 $32 - 12 = 20$
$20 \div 4 = 5$
If there are 5 balls in each of the four corners, each of the remaining boxes contains 3 balls.

Ans 4 Place 4 balls in each box.

Page 16

11. Each term added is a consecutive even number.
$45 + 14 = 59$

12. To find the second term, add the first term and third term together. Divide the result by 3.
$1 + 11 = 12,$
$12 \div 3 = 4$
The same rule applies for the rest of the terms.
$4 + 29 = 33,$
$33 \div 3 = 11$
To find the 8th term, multiply 521 by 3 and subtract 199 from the result.
$521 \times 3 = 1,563$
$1,563 - 199 = 1,364$

13. The rule is to find the square of each term. To square means to multiply the number by itself.
$1 \times 1 = 1$
$2 \times 2 = 4$
$3 \times 3 = 9$
$4 \times 4 = 16$
$5 \times 5 = 25$
$6 \times 6 = 36$

14. The difference between the two terms increases by 1. To get the next term, add the difference to the previous term.
$16 + ⑥ = 22$
$22 + ⑦ = 29$

15. The difference between two terms increases by 2. To get the next term, add the difference to the previous term.
$32 + ⑫ = 44$
$44 + ⑭ = 58$

Page 17

16. Add 1 to the odd terms and 5 to the even terms.
$3 + 1 = 4$
$4 + 5 = 9$
$9 + 1 = 10$
$10 + 5 = 15$
$15 + 1 = 16$
$16 + 5 = 21$
$21 + 1 = 22$

17. Add 2 to the odd terms and multiply the even terms by 2.

1 (+2) = 3
3 (×2) = 6
6 (+2) = 8
8 (×2) = 16
16 (+2) = 18
18 (×2) = 36
36 (+2) = 38

18. All sequences are Fibonacci numbers except for (d).

Page 18

19. (a) In each number pattern, find the difference of the numbers at the top and bottom. Multiply the difference by the number on the left-hand side to get the correct answer.
10 − 7 = 3
6 × 3 = 18

(b) In each number pattern, find the sum of the numbers at the top and bottom. Divide the number on the right-hand side by the sum to get the correct answer.
10 + 2 = 12
36 ÷ 12 = 3

(c) In the first number pattern,
7 + 5 = 12
12 ÷ 4 = 3
The same rule applies.
9 + 7 = 16
16 ÷ 4 = 4

Page 19

20. This is an example of Fibonacci numbers.

Jan.	$10
Feb.	$20
Mar.	$30
Apr.	$50
May.	$80
Jun.	$130
Jul.	$210
Aug.	$340
Sep.	$550
Oct.	$890

(a) She saved $210 in July.
(b) She saved $890 in October.

Page 20

21. Observe the pattern in each row.
The second row is the multiplication table of 2, the third row is the multiplication table of 3 and the fourth row is the multiplication table of 4.
So, the fifth and sixth rows are multiplication tables of 5 and 6 respectively.
5 (10) (15) (20) (25)
6 12 (18) (24) (30) (36) (42)

Solutions

Chapter 2 Practice

Page 24

1. There are 3 pairs of 18.
   3 × 18 = 54
2. There are 3 pairs of 10.
   3 × 10 = 30
   30 + 5 = 35
3. There are 4 pairs of 13.
   4 × 13 = 52
4. There are 3 pairs of 16.
   3 × 16 = 48
   48 + 8 = 56

Page 25

5. There are 4 pairs of 46.
   4 × 46 = 184
6. There are 3 pairs of 18.
   3 × 18 = 54
   Since 9 is not paired up,
   54 + 9 = 63
7. There are 3 pairs of 25.
   3 × 25 = 75
8. There are 3 pairs of 38.
   3 × 38 = 114

Page 26

9. There are 25 pairs of 51.
   25 × 51 = 1,275
10. There are 25 even numbers from 2 to 50 and therefore 12 pairs of 52.
    12 × 52 = 624
    To find the remaining number,
    (50 + 2) ÷ 2 = 26
    624 + 26 = 650
11. There are 25 odd numbers from 1 to 49 and therefore 12 pairs of 50.
    12 × 50 = 600
    To find the remaining number,
    (1 + 49) ÷ 2 = 25
    600 + 25 = 625
12. There are 50 pairs of 101.
    50 × 101 = 5,050

Page 27

13. We have to find the value of 15 + 30 + 45 + 60 + 75 + 90 + 105 + 120.
    4 × 135 = 540
    Cindy saved $540 in all.
14. We have to find the value of 10 + 12 + 14 + 16 + 18 + 20 + 22 + 24 + 26 + 28 + 30 + 32.
    6 × 42 = 252
    There are 252 seats in the cinema altogether.

Page 28

15. We have to find the value of 20 + 25 + 30 + 35 + 40 + 45 + 50 + 55 + 60 + 65 + 70 + 75 + 80.
    6 × 100 = 600
    600 + 50 = 650
    There were 650 pages in the storybook.

Page 29

16. **(a)** Form a number sequence of 16 terms. Start with the largest number, 75, and decrease by 3 each time.
    75 72 69 66 63 60 57 54
    51 48 45 42 39 36 33 30
    There are 30 seats in the first row.
    (b) We have 8 pairs of (75 + 30) = 105
    8 × 105 = 840
    There are 840 seats in the auditorium.
17. Two observations on the sequence:
    (1) The numbers repeat every five numbers.
    (2) The sum of every five numbers, 3 + 3 + 1 + 9 + 4, is 20.
    (a) 33 ÷ 5 = 6 R 3
    The 33rd number is the same as the third number in the pattern. So, it is 1.
    (b) 40 terms is equal to 8 sets of repeating numbers.
    8 × 20 = 160
    The sum of the first 40 terms is 160.

Page 30

18. Since each book was written and published every two years, the years in which the 7 books were written and published were:
1995 1997 1999 2001 2003 2005 2007

19. Find the value of 1 + 2 + 3 + 4 + 5 + 6 + 7 + 8 + 9 + 10.
5 × 11 = 55
In order to have 10 groups of different numbers of tennis balls, there must be 55 tennis balls.
So, it is not possible to group 54 tennis balls into 10 groups of different numbers of tennis balls.

Page 31

20. If player A plays one match against the rest of the players, he or she will play 19 matches. Since player B has already played against A, he or she needs to play only 18 matches against the rest of the players. Player C will play only 17 matches, and so forth. So the number of matches each successive player needs to play will decrease by 1.
In order to find the total number of matches, we find the value of 1 + 2 + 3 + ... + 17 + 18 + 19.
(1 + 19) × 9 = 180
180 + 10 = 190
There are 190 matches in the competition.

21. (a) 12 + 1 + 2 + 3 + 4 + 5 + 6 + 7 + 8 + 9 + 10 + 11
Rearranging the sequence,
1 + 2 + 3 + 4 + 5 + 6 + 7 + 8 + 9 + 10 + 11 + 12
6 × 13 = 78
It will chime 78 times between 12 noon and 11 o'clock at night.

(b) 78 × 2 = 156
It will chime 156 times in 24 hours.

Chapter 3 Practice

Page 39

1. (a)
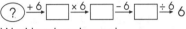
75 ←×3 25 ←−5 30 ←÷2 60

(b)
20 ←÷3 60 ←+4 56 ←×4 14

(c)
13 ←÷2 26 ←−4 30 ←×5 6

Page 40

2. Write down the problem as shown below.
? →+6 □ →×6 □ →−6 □ →÷6 6
Working backward,
1 ←−6 7 ←÷6 42 ←+6 36 ←×6 6
this number is 1.

3. Write down the problem as shown below.
? →+3 □ →×5 □ →−8 12
Working backward,
1 ←−3 4 ←÷5 20 ←+8 12
this number is 1.

Page 41

4.

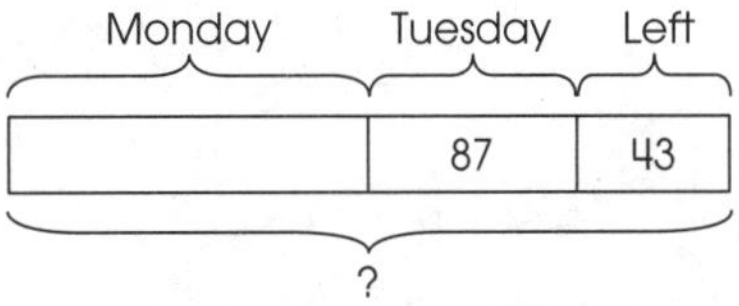

Monday	Tuesday	Left
	87	43

?

87 + 43 = 130
130 × 2 = 260
There were 260 books in the library at first.

5. Write down the problem as shown below.
? →−6 □ →+10 □ →−5 19
20 ←+6 14 ←−10 24 ←+5 19
The white rabbit gathered 20 mushrooms at first.

Page 42

6. Since 4 cars drove away, 36 − 4 = 32 cars were in the two parking lots.

Parking lot A [8][8][8]
Parking lot B [8] } 32

There were 24 cars in parking lot A and 8 cars in parking lot B in the end.

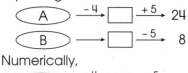

Numerically,

A (23) ←$\overset{+4}{\quad}$ [19] ←$\overset{-5}{\quad}$ 24
B (13) ←$\quad$ [13] ←$\overset{+5}{\quad}$ 8

There were 23 cars in parking lot A and 13 cars in parking lot B at first.

7. Since 2 sparrows flew away,
16 − 2 = 14
there were 14 sparrows left.
14 ÷ 2 = 7
There were 7 sparrows on each tree in the end.

(1st tree) →$\quad$ □ →$\overset{-5}{\quad}$ 7
(2nd tree) →$\overset{-2}{\quad}$ □ →$\overset{+5}{\quad}$ 7

Numerically,

1st tree (12) ←$\quad$ [12] →$\overset{+5}{\quad}$ 7
2nd tree (4) →$\overset{+2}{\quad}$ [2] ←$\overset{-5}{\quad}$ 7

There were 12 sparrows on the first tree and 4 sparrows on the second tree at first.

Page 43

8. Since Cindy had three times as much money as Elaine,

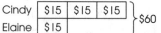

Cindy had $45 and Elaine had $15 in the end.

(Cindy) →$\overset{-12}{\quad}$ □ →$\overset{+10}{\quad}$ 45
(Elaine) →$\overset{+12}{\quad}$ □ →$\overset{-10}{\quad}$ 15

Numerically,

Cindy (47) ←$\overset{+12}{\quad}$ [35] ←$\overset{-10}{\quad}$ 45
Elaine (13) ←$\overset{-12}{\quad}$ [25] ←$\overset{+10}{\quad}$ 15

Cindy had $47 and Elaine had $13 at first.

9. Since the number of marbles in Box A was twice of that in Box B,

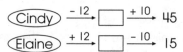

there were 60 marbles in Box A and 30 marbles in Box B in the end.

(Box A) →$\overset{-15}{\quad}$ □ →$\overset{+18}{\quad}$ 60
(Box B) →$\overset{+15}{\quad}$ □ →$\overset{-18}{\quad}$ 30

Numerically,

Box A (57) ←$\overset{+15}{\quad}$ [42] ←$\overset{-18}{\quad}$ 60
Box B (33) ←$\overset{-15}{\quad}$ [48] ←$\overset{+18}{\quad}$ 30

There were 57 marbles in Box A and 33 marbles in Box B at first.

978-1-62399-074-9
Singapore Math Challenge

Page 44

10. Since 2 flying squirrels from each branch flew away,

$16 - 2 - 2 = 12$

only 12 flying squirrels remained on the tree.

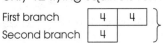

First branch [4 | 4] } 12
Second branch [4]

8 flying squirrels were resting on the first branch and 4 flying squirrels were resting on the second branch in the end.

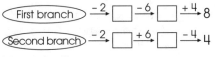

First branch $\xrightarrow{-2}$ □ $\xrightarrow{-6}$ □ $\xrightarrow{+4}$ 8

Second branch $\xrightarrow{-2}$ □ $\xrightarrow{+6}$ □ $\xrightarrow{-4}$ 4

Numerically,

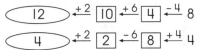

12 $\xrightarrow{\div 2}$ [10] $\xrightarrow{+6}$ [4] $\xrightarrow{-4}$ 8

4 $\xrightarrow{\div 2}$ [2] $\xrightarrow{-6}$ [8] $\xrightarrow{+4}$ 4

12 flying squirrels and 4 flying squirrels were on the first and second branches respectively at first.

Page 45

11.

? $\xrightarrow{+4}$ □ $\xrightarrow{-6}$ □ $\xrightarrow{\times 2}$ □ $\xrightarrow{-3}$ 15

11 $\xleftarrow{-4}$ [15] $\xleftarrow{+6}$ [9] $\xleftarrow{\div 2}$ [18] $\xleftarrow{+3}$ 15

11 commuters were on the bus when it left the bus terminal.

12.

? floor $\xrightarrow{+4}$ □ $\xrightarrow{-3}$ □ $\xrightarrow{-3}$ 6

8th floor $\xleftarrow{-4}$ [12] $\xleftarrow{+3}$ [9] $\xleftarrow{+3}$ 6

Debra's apartment is on the 8th floor.

Page 46

13.

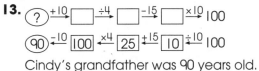

? $\xrightarrow{+10}$ □ $\xrightarrow{\div 4}$ □ $\xrightarrow{-15}$ □ $\xrightarrow{\times 10}$ 100

90 $\xleftarrow{-10}$ [100] $\xleftarrow{\times 4}$ [25] $\xleftarrow{+15}$ [10] $\xleftarrow{\div 10}$ 100

Cindy's grandfather was 90 years old.

14.

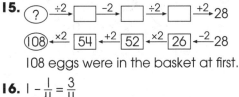

? $\xrightarrow{\div 2}$ □ $\xrightarrow{\div 2}$ □ $\xrightarrow{\div 2}$ □ $\xrightarrow{\div 2}$ 1

16 $\xleftarrow{\times 2}$ [8] $\xleftarrow{\times 2}$ [4] $\xleftarrow{\times 2}$ [2] $\xleftarrow{\times 2}$ 1

The original length of the rope was 16 m.

Page 47

15.

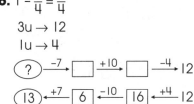

? $\xrightarrow{\div 2}$ □ $\xrightarrow{-2}$ □ $\xrightarrow{\div 2}$ □ $\xrightarrow{+2}$ 28

108 $\xleftarrow{\times 2}$ [54] $\xleftarrow{+2}$ [52] $\xleftarrow{\times 2}$ [26] $\xleftarrow{-2}$ 28

108 eggs were in the basket at first.

16. $1 - \dfrac{1}{4} = \dfrac{3}{4}$

$3u \rightarrow 12$

$1u \rightarrow 4$

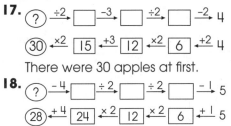

? $\xrightarrow{-7}$ □ $\xrightarrow{+10}$ □ $\xrightarrow{-4}$ 12

13 $\xleftarrow{+7}$ [6] $\xleftarrow{-10}$ [16] $\xleftarrow{+4}$ 12

13 passengers were on the minivan when it left the condominium.

Page 48

17.

? $\xrightarrow{\div 2}$ □ $\xrightarrow{-3}$ □ $\xrightarrow{\div 2}$ □ $\xrightarrow{-2}$ 4

30 $\xleftarrow{\times 2}$ [15] $\xleftarrow{+3}$ [12] $\xleftarrow{\times 2}$ [6] $\xleftarrow{+2}$ 4

There were 30 apples at first.

18.

? $\xrightarrow{-4}$ □ $\xrightarrow{\div 2}$ □ $\xrightarrow{\div 2}$ □ $\xrightarrow{-1}$ 5

28 $\xleftarrow{+4}$ [24] $\xleftarrow{\times 2}$ [12] $\xleftarrow{\times 2}$ [6] $\xleftarrow{+1}$ 5

Alice had $28 at first.

978-1-62399-074-9
Singapore Math Challenge

Page 49

19. $90 \div 3 = \$30$

Each boy had $30 in the end.

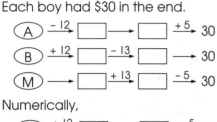

Numerically,

A ⟨37⟩ ←$^{+12}$ ⟨25⟩ ← ⟨25⟩ ←$^{-5}$ 30

B ⟨31⟩ ←$^{-12}$ ⟨43⟩ →$^{+13}$ ⟨30⟩ ← 30

M ⟨22⟩ ← ⟨22⟩ ←$^{-13}$ ⟨35⟩ ←$^{+5}$ 30

Alex had $37, Benny had $31 and Mike had $22 at first.

20. $90 \div 3 = 30$

Each girl has 30 books in the end.

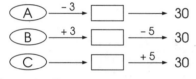

Numerically,

A ⟨33⟩ ←$^{+3}$ ⟨30⟩ ← 30

B ⟨32⟩ ←$^{-3}$ ⟨35⟩ →$^{+5}$ 30

C ⟨25⟩ ← ⟨25⟩ ←$^{-5}$ 30

Alicia has 33 books, Betty has 32 books and Chloe has 25 books at first.

Chapter 4 Practice

Page 58

1. *Method 1: Make a Table*

Start with half the total for each vehicle.

No. of cars	No. of wheels	No. of motorcycles	No. of wheels	Total no. of wheels
15	60	15	30	90

The total number of wheels should be 100.

$100 - 90 = 10$ (difference in total number of wheels)

$4 - 2 = 2$ (difference in the number of wheels between the two vehicles)

$10 \div 2 = 5$ (add 5 cars and subtract 5 motorcyles to the first guess)

No. of cars	No. of wheels	No. of motorcycles	No. of wheels	Total no. of wheels
20	80	10	20	100

There were 20 cars at the parking lot.

Method 2: Make an Assumption

If all were motorcycles,

$30 \times 2 = 60$

there would be 60 wheels.

$100 - 60 = 40$

There is a difference of 40 wheels.

$4 - 2 = 2$

The difference of the number of wheels between a car and a motorcycle is 2.

$40 \div 2 = 20$

There were 20 cars at the parking lot.

978-1-62399-074-9
Singapore Math Challenge

Page 59

2. *Method 1: Make a Table*

Start with half the total for each type of ticket.

No. of audit tickets	Value	No. of child tickets	Value	Total value
5	$40	5	$25	$65

The total cost of all the movie tickets should be $74.

$74 – $65 = $9 (difference in total cost of the movie tickets)

$8 – $5 = $3 (difference between the adult and child movie tickets)

$9 ÷ $3 = 3 (add 3 adult movie tickets and subtract 3 child movie tickets to the first guess)

No. of adult tickets	Value	No. of child tickets	Value	Total value
8	$64	2	$10	$74

Sean buys 8 adult movie tickets and 2 child movie tickets.

Method 2: Make an Assumption

If all were adult movie tickets,

10 × $8 = $80

Sean would have to pay $80.

$80 – $74 = $6

There is a difference of $6.

$8 – $5 = $3

$6 ÷ $3 = 2

Sean buys 2 child movie tickets.

10 – 2 = 8

Sean buys 8 adult movie tickets.

OR

If all were child movie tickets,

10 × $5 = $50

Sean would have to pay $50.

$74 – $50 = $24

There is a difference of $24.

$8 – $5 = $3

$24 ÷ $3 = 8

Sean buys 8 adult movie tickets.

10 – 8 = 2

Sean buys 2 child movie tickets.

Page 60

3. *Method 1: Make a Table*

Start with half the total for each type of stamp.

No. of 50¢ stamps	Value	No. of 20¢ stamps	Value	Total value
15	$7.50	15	$3	$10.50

The total value of the stamps should be $12.

$12 – $10.50 = $1.50 (difference in total value of stamps)

50¢ – 20¢ = 30¢ (difference between the 50¢ and 20¢ stamps)

$1.50 ÷ 30¢ = 5 (add five 50¢ stamps and subtract five 20¢ stamps to the first guess)

No. of 50¢ stamps	Value	No. of 20¢ stamps	Value	Total value
20	$10	10	$2	$12

Clifford has 20 50¢ stamps and 10 20¢ stamps.

Method 2: Make an Assumption

If all were 50¢ stamps,

30 × 50¢ = $15

the total value of all his stamps would be $15.

$15 – $12 = $3

There is a difference of $3.

50¢ – 20¢ = 30¢

$3 ÷ 30¢ = 10

Clifford has 10 20¢ stamps.

30 – 10 = 20

Clifford has 20 50¢ stamps.

OR

If all were 20¢ stamps,

30 × 20¢ = $6

the total value of all his stamps would be $6.

$12 – $6 = $6

There is a difference of $6.

50¢ – 20¢ = 30¢

$6 ÷ 30¢ = 20

Clifford has 20 50¢ stamps.

30 – 20 = 10

Clifford has 10 20¢ stamps.

© Singapore Asia Publishers Pte Ltd

978-1-62399-074-9
Singapore Math Challenge

Page 61

4. *Method 1: Make a Table*

Start with half the total for both the spiders and dragonflies.

No. of spiders	No. of legs	No. of dragonflies	No. of legs	Total no. of legs
10	80	10	60	140

There should be 144 legs in all.

144 – 140 = 4 (difference in total number of legs)

8 – 6 = 2 (difference between the number of legs of a spider and a dragonfly)

4 ÷ 2 = 2 (add 2 spiders and subtract 2 dragonflies to the first guess)

No. of spiders	No. of legs	No. of dragonflies	No. of legs	Total no. of legs
12	96	8	48	144

The number of spiders and dragonflies are 12 and 8 respectively.

Method 2: Make an Assumption

If all were spiders,

20 × 8 = 160

the total number of legs would be 160.

160 – 144 = 16

There is a difference of 16 legs.

8 – 6 = 2

16 ÷ 2 = 8

The number of dragonflies is 8.

20 – 8 = 12

The number of spiders is 12.

OR

If all were dragonflies,

20 × 6 = 120

the total number of legs would be 120.

144 – 120 = 24

There is a difference of 24 legs.

8 – 6 = 2

24 ÷ 2 = 12

The number of spiders is 12.

20 – 12 = 8

The number of dragonflies is 8.

Page 62

5. *Method 1: Make a Table*

Start with half the total for each type of bill.

No. of $5 bills	Value	No. of $10 bills	Value	Total value
15	$75	15	$150	$225

Her total savings should be $220.

$225 – $220 = $5 (difference in total savings)

$10 – $5 = $5 (difference between the value of $5 and $10 bills)

$5 ÷ $5 = 1 (add one $5 bill and subtract one $10 bill to the first guess)

No. of $5 bills	Value	No. of $10 bills	Value	Total value
16	$80	14	$140	$220

Natalie has fourteen $10 bills.

Method 2: Make an Assumption

If all 30 bills were $5 bills,

30 × $5 = $150

the total value would be $150.

$220 – $150 = $70

There is a difference of $70 in the total value.

$10 – $5 = $5

$70 ÷ $5 = 14

Natalie has fourteen $10 bills.

Page 63

6. If we assume Amy answers all questions correctly,
$5 \times 30 = 150$
she will score 150 points.
$150 - 122 = 28$
There is a difference of 28 between the full points and Amy's score.
$5 + 2 = 7$
Amy will lose 7 points if she gets a wrong answer.
$28 \div 7 = 4$
$30 - 4 = 26$
She answers 26 questions correctly.

7. If we assume Henry had answered all questions correctly,
$4 \times 45 = 180$
he would score 180 points.
$180 - 150 = 30$
There is a difference of 30 between the full points and Henry's score.
$4 + 2 = 6$
Henry would lose 6 points if he got a wrong answer.
$30 \div 6 = 5$
He had answered 5 questions wrongly.

Page 64

8. $2 + 1 = 3$
An adult and a child take 3 slices of bread.
$99 \div 3 = 33$
All the children take 33 slices of bread.
$33 \times 2 = 66$
All the adults take 66 slices of bread.
$66 \div 2 = 33$
(a) There are 33 adults.
$33 \div 1 = 33$
(b) There are 33 children.

9. $3 + 1 = 4$
An adult and 3 children could consume 4 buns.
$100 \div 4 = 25$
There were 25 adults.

Page 65

10. *Method 1: Make a Table*

No. of big boats	No. of people	No. of small boats	No. of people	Total no. of people
2	16	7	40	56
4	32	4	24	56
6	48	2	8	56
7	56	0	0	56

As the total number of boats is not stated in this question, we can only use the guess-and-check method. Not surprisingly, we have many sets of possible answers.

Method 2: Make an Assumption
If all were big boats,
$56 \div 8 = 7$
there would be 7 big boats.
Alternative Assumption
It is not possible to hire all small boats as 56 is not divisible by 6.

Page 66

11. If all the questions are answered correctly,

$20 \times 8 = 160$

Isabella will score 160 points.

$160 - 100 = 60$

There is a difference of 60 between the full points and Isabella's score.

$8 + 4 = 12$

She will lose 12 points if she gets a wrong answer.

$60 \div 12 = 5$

$20 - 5 = 15$

She answers 15 questions correctly.

12. If all were volleyballs,

$4 + 5 = 9$

there would be 9 volleyballs.

$\$8 \times 4 = \$32$

$\$230 - \$32 = \$198$

9 volleyballs cost $198.

$\$198 \div 9 = \$22$

The cost of each volleyball was $22.

$\$22 + \$8 = \$30$

The cost of each basketball was $30.

Page 67

13. *Method 1: Make a Table*

Start with half the total for each type of stationery.

No. of pens	Cost	No. of books	Cost	Total cost
5	$20	5	$35	$55

The total cost should be $64.

$\$64 - \$55 = \$9$ (difference in total cost)

$\quad \$7 - \$4 = \$3$ (difference between the cost of a pen and a book)

$\quad \$9 \div \$3 = 3$ (add 3 books and subtract 3 pens to the first guess)

No. of pens	Cost	No. of books	Cost	Total cost
2	$8	8	$56	$64

He had bought 2 pens and 8 books.

Method 2: Make an Assumption

If all were pens,

$\$4 \times 10 = \$40$

Samuel would pay $40.

$\$64 - \$40 = \$24$

There is a difference of $24.

$\$7 - \$4 = \$3$

$\$24 \div \$3 = 8$

He had bought 8 books.

$10 - 8 = 2$

He had bought 2 pens.

OR

If all were books,

$\$7 \times 10 = \$70$

Samuel would pay $70.

$\$70 - \$64 = \$6$

There is a difference of $6.

$\$7 - \$4 = \$3$

$\$6 \div \$3 = 2$

He had bought 2 pens.

$10 - 2 = 8$

He had bought 8 books.

Page 68

14. *Method 1: Make a Table*

Start with half the total for each type.

No. of whiteboard markers	Value	No. of paintbrushes	Value	Total Value
6	$18	6	$6	$24

The total cost should be $28.

$28 – $24 = $4 (difference in total cost)

$3 – $1 = $2 (difference between the value of a whiteboard marker and a paintbrush)

$4 ÷ $2 = 2 (add 2 whiteboard markers and subtract 2 paintbrushes to the first guess)

No. of whiteboard markers	Value	No. of paintbrushes	Value	Total Value
8	$24	4	$4	$28

The teacher bought 8 whiteboard markers and 4 paintbrushes.

Method 2: Make an Assumption

If all were whiteboard markers,

$3 × 12 = $36

the teacher would pay $36.

$36 – $28 = $8

There is a difference of $8 in the total value.

$3 – $1 = $2

$8 ÷ $2 = 4

The teacher bought 4 paintbrushes.

12 – 4 = 8

The teacher bought 8 whiteboard markers.

OR

If all were paintbrushes,

$1 × 12 = $12

the teacher would pay $12.

$28 – $12 = $16

There is a difference of $16.

$3 – $1 = $2

$16 ÷ $2 = 8

The teacher bought 8 whiteboard markers.

12 – 8 = 4

The teacher bought 4 paintbrushes.

Chapter 5 Practice

Page 74

1. number of intervals

= 900 m ÷ 15 m

= 60

60 + 1 = 61

61 trees are to be planted along that stretch of road.

2. number of intervals

= 150 m ÷ 5 m

= 30

30 + 1 = 31

31 pine trees are needed to be planted along the road.

Page 75

3. number of intervals

= 1800 m ÷ 30 m

= 60

60 + 1 = 61

61 lamp posts are placed along the road.

4. number of intervals

= number of students – 1

= 12 – 1

= 11

4 × 11 = 44

There are 44 pots of flowers altogether.

Page 76

5. number of staircases from the ground floor to the fifth floor

= 5 – 1

= 4

80 steps ÷ 4 = 20 steps

There were 20 steps in each staircase.

number of staircases from the ground floor to the sixth floor

= 6 – 1

= 5

5 × 20 steps = 100 steps

Maurice walked 100 steps from the ground floor to his house.

978-1-62399-074-9
Singapore Math Challenge

6. number of intervals from the first tree to the sixth tree
= 6 – 1
= 5
10 ÷ 5 = 2
Benny takes 2 min. to walk from one tree to another.
number of intervals from the first tree to the fifteenth tree
= 15 – 1
= 14
2 × 14 = 28
It takes 28 min. for him to walk to the fifteenth tree.

Page 77

7. At 3 pm, there are only 2 intervals between the first and third chimes.
6 sec. ÷ 2 = 3 sec.
It takes 3 sec. to chime once.
At 6 pm, there are only 5 intervals between the first and sixth chimes.
5 × 3 sec. = 15 sec.
The grandfather clock takes 15 sec. to chime 6 times at 6 pm.

8. number of intervals
= number of trees – 1
= 95 – 1
= 94
94 × 5 m = 470 m
The road was 470 m long.

Page 78

9. 38 ÷ 2 = 19
There were 19 students in each row.
number of intervals
= number of students – 1
= 19 – 1
= 18
18 × 50 cm = 900 cm
The length of the line was 900 cm or 9 m.

10. 48 ÷ 2 = 24
There are 24 students in each row.
number of intervals = 24 – 1 = 23
23 × 1 m = 23 m
The line is 23 m long.

Page 79

11. number of intervals = 100 – 1 = 99
99 × 6 m = 594 m
The road is 594 m long.

12. number of intervals = 9 + 1 = 10
100 m ÷ 10 = 10 m
The distance between each tree is 10 m.

Page 80

13. number of intervals = 79 + 1 = 80
320 m ÷ 80 = 4 m
The distance between each tree is 4 m.

14. number of intervals = 40 ÷ 2 = 20
number of pots of plants = 20 – 1 = 19
There are 19 pots of plants.

Page 81

15. In the case of circular tracks,
number of intervals = number of trees
$600 \div 6 = 100$
100 trees are planted around the lake.

16. *Method 1: Solve Using Drawing*
From the above diagram,

$4 \times 4 = 16$
$16 + 4 = 20$

there are 20 flowers on the handkerchief altogether.

Method 2: Solve By Reasoning
If the number of flowers on each side is multiplied by four sides, you will have four extra flowers as the flowers on the four corners are counted twice.
$6 \times 4 = 24$
$24 - 4 = 20$
There are 20 flowers on the handkerchief altogether.

Page 82

17. *Method 1: Solve Using Drawing*
From the diagram,
$4 \times 3 = 12$
$12 + 3 = 15$
15 coins were used to make the triangle.

Method 2: Solve By Reasoning
If the number of coins on each side is multiplied by three, you will have an extra three coins as the coins on the three corners are counted twice.
$3 \times 6 = 18$
$18 - 3 = 15$
15 coins were used to make the triangle.

18. number of intervals = $11 - 1 = 10$
10 min. $\div$ 10 = 1 min.
30 min. $\div$ 1 min. = 30 intervals
$30 + 1 = 31$
Uncle Sam would be at the thirty-first lamp post.

Page 83

19. number of intervals
= number of plum trees – 1
= $41 - 1$
= 40
Length of the road
= 4 m $\times$ 40
= 160 m
Number of intervals
= 160 m $\div$ 5 m
= 32
$32 + 1 = 33$
There are 33 pine trees on this side of the road.

20. Number of intervals in each row
= 20 m $\div$ 1 m
= 20
Number of performers in each row
= 20 + 1
= 21
$5 \times 21 = 105$
There are 105 performers altogether.

Chapter 6 Practice

Page 87,88,89

1. **(a)** $23 + 99 = 23 + 100 - 1$
$$= 123 - 1$$
$$= 122$$

(b) $152 - 97 = 152 - 100 + 3$
$$= 52 + 3$$
$$= 55$$

(c) $162 - 97 = 162 - 100 + 3$
$$= 62 + 3$$
$$= 65$$

(d) $565 - 298 = 565 - 300 + 2$
$$= 265 + 2$$
$$= 267$$

(e) $638 + 397 = 638 + 400 - 3$
$$= 1,038 - 3$$
$$= 1,035$$

(f) $499 + 127 = 500 + 127 - 1$
$$= 627 - 1$$
$$= 626$$

(g) $645 - 98 = 645 - 100 + 2$
$$= 545 + 2$$
$$= 547$$

(h) $533 - 199 = 533 - 200 + 1$
$$= 333 + 1$$
$$= 334$$

(i) $285 + 297 = 285 + 300 - 3$
$$= 585 - 3$$
$$= 582$$

(j) $424 - 196 = 424 - 200 + 4$
$$= 224 + 4$$
$$= 228$$

(k) $43 + 99 + 58 = 40 + (99 + 1) + (58 + 2)$
$$= 40 + 100 + 60$$
$$= 200$$

(l) $56 + 87 + 77 = 50 + (3 + 87) + (3 + 77)$
$$= 50 + 90 + 80$$
$$= 20 + (10 + 90) + (20 + 80)$$
$$= 220$$

(m) $74 + 75 + 28 = 74 + 3 + (75 + 25)$
$$= 77 + 100$$
$$= 177$$

(n) $27 + 86 + 63 + 14 = 27 + 63 + (86 + 14)$
$$= 90 + 100$$
$$= 190$$

(o) $323 + 677 + 92 + 108$
$$= (323 + 677) + 92 + 108$$
$$= 1,000 + 200$$
$$= 1,200$$

(p) $167 + 355 + 345 + 133$
$$= 167 + 133 + 355 + 345$$
$$= 300 + 700$$
$$= 1,000$$

(q) $9,999 + 999 + 99 + 9$
$$= (10,000 - 1) + (1,000 - 1) + (100 - 1) + (10 - 1)$$
$$= 10,000 + 1,000 + 100 + 10 - 4$$
$$= 11,106$$

(r) $18 + 28 + 38 + 48 + 58$
$$= (20 - 2) + (30 - 2) + (40 - 2) + (50 - 2) + (60 - 2)$$
$$= 200 - 10$$
$$= 190$$

(s) $9,997 + 4 + 99 + 998 + 3 + 9$
$$= (9,997 + 3) + (1 + 99) + (998 + 2) + (1 + 9)$$
$$= 10,000 + 100 + 1,000 + 10$$
$$= 11,110$$

(t) $74 + 75 + 77 + 80 + 82 + 85$
$$= 71 + (3 + 77) + 80 + 80 + 2 + 80 + (5 + 75)$$
$$= 71 + 2 + 80 + 80 + 80 + 80 + 80$$
$$= 73 + 400$$
$$= 473$$

(u) 299,999 + 29,999 + 2,999 + 299 + 29
= (300,000 − 1) + (30,000 − 1) + (3,000 − 1) +
(300 − 1) + (30 − 1)
= 333,330 − 5
= 333,325

(v) 133 + 135 + 140 + 147 + 145 + 142 + 138
= 140 + (133 + 7) + 140 + (135 + 5) + 140 +
140 + (2 + 138)
= 140 × 7
= 980

Page 90,91

2. **(a)** 420 − 102 − 98
= 420 − (102 + 98)
= 420 − 200
= 220

(b) 240 − 104 − 96
= 240 − (104 + 96)
= 240 − 200
= 40

(c) 325 − 10 − 20 − 80 − 90
= 325 − (10 + 90 + 20 + 80)
= 325 − 200
= 125

(d) 400 − 90 − 80 − 20 − 10 − 5
= 400 − (90 + 10 + 80 + 20) − 5
= 400 − 200 − 5
= 195

(e) 235 − 15 − 25 − 75 − 85
= 235 − (15 + 85 + 25 + 75)
= 235 − 200
= 35

(f) 200 − 1 − 2 − 3 − 4 − 5
= 200 − (1 + 2 + 3 + 4 + 5)
= 200 − 15
= 185

(g) 120 − 117 + 116 − 113 + 112 − 109 + ⋯ + 100
− 97
120 − 117 = 3
116 − 113 = 3
112 − 109 = 3
100 − 97 = 3
Every subtraction pair has a difference of 3.
Count the minuends, 100, 104, 108, 112,
116, 120.
3 + 3 + 3 + 3 + 3 + 3 = 18
The answer is 18.

(h) 145 − 141 + 140 − 136 + 135 − 131 + ⋯ + 95 −
91
145 − 141 = 4
140 − 136 = 4
135 − 131 = 4
95 − 91 = 4
Every subtraction pair has a difference of 4.
Count the minuends, 95, 100, 105, 110,
115, 120, 125, 130, 135, 140, 145.
4 + 4 + 4 + 4 + 4 + 4 + 4 + 4 + 4 + 4 + 4 = 44
The answer is 44.

(i) 800 − 10 − 20 − 30 − 40 − 50 − 60 − 70 − 80 − 90
= 800 − (10 + 90 + 20 + 80 + 30 + 70 + 40 +
60 + 50)
= 800 − (100 + 100 + 100 + 100 + 50)
= 800 − 450
= 350

Page 92,93,94,95

3. **(a)** 375 + 286 + 125 + 714
= (375 + 125) + (286 + 714)
= 500 + 1,000
= 1,500

(b) 728 + 140 + 272
= (728 + 272) + 140
= 1,000 + 140
= 1,140

(c) $37 + 97 + 3{,}997 + 99$
$= (40 - 3) + (100 - 3) + (4{,}000 - 3) + (100 - 1)$
$= 4{,}240 - 10$
$= 4{,}230$

(d) $71 + 69 + 68 + 73 + 74$
$= 70 + (1 + 69) + (68 + 2) + 70 + 1 + 70 + 4$
$= 70 + 70 + 70 + 70 + 70 + 5$
$= 350 + 5$
$= 355$

(e) $1{,}897 + 128 - 597$
$= 1{,}897 - 597 + 128$
$= 1{,}300 + 128$
$= 1{,}428$

(f) $728 - (28 + 320)$
$= 728 - 28 - 320$
$= 700 - 320$
$= 380$

(g) $1{,}290 - 164 - 736$
$= 1{,}290 - (164 + 736)$
$= 1{,}290 - 900$
$= 390$

(h) $1{,}330 - 288 - 342$
$= 1{,}330 - (288 + 342)$
$= 1{,}330 - 630$
$= 700$

(i) $843 + 78 - 43$
$= 843 - 43 + 78$
$= 800 + 78$
$= 878$

(j) $528 - (186 + 328)$
$= 528 - 328 - 186$
$= 200 - 186$
$= 14$

(k) $564 - (387 - 136)$
$= 564 + 136 - 387$
$= 700 - 387$
$= 313$

(l) $847 - 578 + 398 - 222$
$= 847 - (578 + 222) + 398$
$= 847 - 800 + (400 - 2)$
$= 47 + 400 - 2$
$= 445$

(m) $936 - 867 - 99 + 267$
$= 936 - (100 - 1) - (867 - 267)$
$= 936 - 100 - 600 + 1$
$= 236 + 1$
$= 237$

(n) $33 + 87 + 67 + 13$
$= (33 + 67) + (87 + 13)$
$= 100 + 100$
$= 200$

(o) $96 + 103 + 97 + 104 + 101 + 99$
$= (96 + 104) + (103 + 97) + (101 + 99)$
$= 200 + 200 + 200$
$= 600$

(p) $23 + 56 + 77 + 18 + 44 + 82$
$= (23 + 77) + (56 + 44) + (18 + 82)$
$= 100 + 100 + 100$
$= 300$

(q) $9 + 99 + 999 + 9{,}999$
$= (10 - 1) + (100 - 1) + (1{,}000 - 1) + (10{,}000 - 1)$
$= 10 + 100 + 1{,}000 + 10{,}000 - 4$
$= 11{,}110 - 4$
$= 11{,}106$

(r) $8 + 98 + 998 + 9{,}998$
$= (10 - 2) + (100 - 2) + (1{,}000 - 2) + (10{,}000 - 2)$
$= 10 + 100 + 1{,}000 + 10{,}000 - 8$
$= 11{,}110 - 8$
$= 11{,}102$

(s) $464 - 548 + 99 + 348$
$= 464 + (100 - 1) - (548 - 348)$
$= 564 - 1 - 200$
$= 364 - 1$
$= 363$

(t) $537 - (543 - 163) - 57$
$= 537 - 543 + 163 - 57$
$= (537 + 163) - (543 + 57)$
$= 700 - 600$
$= 100$

(u) $713 - (513 - 229) = 713 - 513 + 229$
$= 200 + 229$
$= 429$

(v) $850 - 486 - 114 = 850 - (486 + 114)$
$= 850 - 600$
$= 250$

(w) $46 + 37 + 54 + 63 = (46 + 54) + (37 + 63)$
$= 100 + 100$
$= 200$

(x) $947 + (372 - 447) - 572$
$= 947 + 372 - 447 - 572$
$= (947 - 447) - (572 - 372)$
$= 500 - 200$
$= 300$

(y) $989 - 675 - 189 = (989 - 189) - 675$
$= 800 - 675$
$= 125$

(z) $583 - 297 - 183 = (583 - 183) - 297$
$= 400 - 297$
$= 103$

Page 95

4. $360 - 357 + 354 - 351 + \cdots + 300 - 297$
$360 - 357 = 3$
$354 - 351 = 3$
$300 - 297 = 3$
Every subtraction pair has a difference of 3.
Count the minuends, 300, 306, 312, 318, 324,
330, 336, 342, 348, 354, 360
$3 + 3 + 3 + 3 + 3 + 3 + 3 + 3 + 3 + 3 + 3 = 33$
The answer is 33.

Chapter 7 Practice

Page 104, 105

I. **(a)** $14 \times 25 \times 4 = 14 \times 100$
$= 1,400$

(b) $4 \times 17 \times 25 = 17 \times 4 \times 25$
$= 17 \times 100$
$= 1,700$

(c) $25 \times 32 \times 125 = 25 \times 4 \times 8 \times 125$
$= 100 \times 1,000$
$= 100,000$

(d) $125 \times 25 \times 4 = 125 \times 100$
$= 12,500$

(e) $56 \times 125 = 7 \times 8 \times 125$
$= 7 \times 1,000$
$= 7,000$

(f) $125 \times 72 = 125 \times 8 \times 9$
$= 1,000 \times 9$
$= 9,000$

(g) $64 \times 5 \times 25 \times 125$
$= 2 \times 4 \times 8 \times 5 \times 25 \times 125$
$= (2 \times 5) \times (4 \times 25) \times (8 \times 125)$
$= 10 \times 100 \times 1,000$
$= 1,000,000$

(h) $56 \times 25 \times 2 \times 5$
$= 14 \times (4 \times 25) \times (2 \times 5)$
$= 14 \times 100 \times 10$
$= 14,000$

(i) $25 \times 16 \times 125 \times 4 \times 5$
$= 25 \times 8 \times 2 \times 125 \times 4 \times 5$
$= (25 \times 4) \times (8 \times 125) \times (2 \times 5)$
$= 100 \times 1,000 \times 10$
$= 1,000,000$

(j) $25 \times 64 \times 125 \times 25$
$= 25 \times 8 \times 8 \times 125 \times 25$
$= (25 \times 4) \times 2 \times (8 \times 125) \times 25$
$= 100 \times 50 \times 1,000$
$= 5,000,000$

(k) $25 \times 24 \times 8 \times 125$
   $= (25 \times 4) \times 6 \times (8 \times 125)$
   $= 100 \times 6 \times 1{,}000$
   $= 600{,}000$

(l) $25 \times 40 \times 125 \times 8$
   $= (25 \times 4) \times 10 \times (125 \times 8)$
   $= 100 \times 10 \times 1{,}000$
   $= 1{,}000{,}000$

Page 106

2-1. (a) $24 = 4 \times 6$
   $= 2 \times 2 \times 2 \times 3$

(b) $36 = 6 \times 6$
   $= 2 \times 3 \times 2 \times 3$
   $= 2 \times 2 \times 3 \times 3$

(c) $27 = 3 \times 9$
   $= 3 \times 3 \times 3$

(d) $44 = 4 \times 11$
   $= 2 \times 2 \times 11$

(e) $42 = 6 \times 7$
   $= 2 \times 3 \times 7$

(f) $56 = 7 \times 8$
   $= 2 \times 2 \times 2 \times 7$

(g) $33 = 3 \times 11$

(h) $64 = 8 \times 8$
   $= 2 \times 2 \times 2 \times 2 \times 2 \times 2$

(i) $48 = 8 \times 6$
   $= 2 \times 2 \times 2 \times 2 \times 3$

(j) $99 = 9 \times 11$
   $= 3 \times 3 \times 11$

Page 107

2-2. (a) $90 = 2 \times 3 \times 3 \times 5$

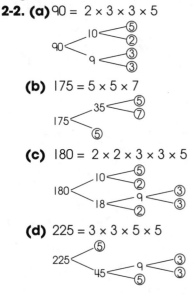

(b) $175 = 5 \times 5 \times 7$

(c) $180 = 2 \times 2 \times 3 \times 3 \times 5$

(d) $225 = 3 \times 3 \times 5 \times 5$

Page 108,109,110

3. (a) $7 \times 14 + 7 \times 86$
   $= 7 \times (14 + 86)$
   $= 7 \times 100$
   $= 700$

(b) $65 \div 11 + 56 \div 11$
   $= (65 + 56) \div 11$
   $= 121 \div 11$
   $= 11$

(c) $24 \times 23 + 24 \times 77$
   $= 24 \times (23 + 77)$
   $= 24 \times 100$
   $= 2{,}400$

(d) $31 \times 84 + 31 \times 16$
   $= 31 \times (84 + 16)$
   $= 31 \times 100$
   $= 3{,}100$

(e) $58 \div 12 + 86 \div 12$
   $= (58 + 86) \div 12$
   $= 144 \div 12$
   $= 12$

(f) $100 \div 14 + 96 \div 14$
   $= (100 + 96) \div 14$
   $= 196 \div 14$
   $= 14$

(g) 35×202
   $= 35 \times (200 + 2)$
   $= (35 \times 200) + (35 \times 2)$
   $= 7{,}000 + 70$
   $= 7{,}070$

(h) 45×98
   $= 45 \times (100 - 2)$
   $= (45 \times 100) - (45 \times 2)$
   $= 4{,}500 - 90$
   $= 4{,}410$

(i) 72×101
$= 72 \times (100 + 1)$
$= (72 \times 100) + (72 \times 1)$
$= 7,200 + 72$
$= 7,272$

(j) 38×99
$= 38 \times (100 - 1)$
$= (38 \times 100) - 38 \times 1$
$= 3,800 - 38$
$= 3,762$

(k) 33×97
$= 33 \times (100 - 3)$
$= (33 \times 100) - (33 \times 3)$
$= 3,300 - 99$
$= 3,201$

(l) 83×99
$= 83 \times (100 - 1)$
$= (83 \times 100) - (83 \times 1)$
$= 8,300 - 83$
$= 8,217$

(m) $4 \times (72 \times 25 + 28 \times 25)$
$= (4 \times 25) \times 72 + (4 \times 25) \times 28$
$= 100 \times 72 + 100 \times 28$
$= 100 \times (72 + 28)$
$= 100 \times 100$
$= 10,000$

(n) $(110 + 25 - 9) \times 8$
$= (110 + 16) \times 8$
$= 126 \times 8$
$= (125 + 1) \times 8$
$= (125 \times 8) + (1 \times 8)$
$= 1,000 + 8$
$= 1,008$

(o) $125 \times (84 \times 8 + 16 \times 8)$
$= 125 \times 84 \times 8 + 125 \times 16 \times 8$
$= 1,000 \times 84 + 1,000 \times 16$
$= 1,000 \times (84 + 16)$
$= 1,000 \times 100$
$= 100,000$

(p) $8 \times (98 - 48 + 74)$
$= 8 \times (50 + 74)$
$= 8 \times 124$
$= 8 \times (125 - 1)$
$= (8 \times 125) - (8 \times 1)$
$= 1,000 - 8$
$= 992$

(q) $25 \times (28 \times 4 + 72 \times 4)$
$= 25 \times 28 \times 4 + 25 \times 72 \times 4$
$= 100 \times 28 + 100 \times 72$
$= 100 \times (28 + 72)$
$= 100 \times 100$
$= 10,000$

(r) $25 \times 73 + 50 \times 73 + 25 \times 73$
$= 73 \times (25 + 50 + 25)$
$= 73 \times 100$
$= 7,300$

(s) $74 + 5 \times 740 + 49 \times 74$
$= 74 + 5 \times 10 \times 74 + 49 \times 74$
$= 74 + 50 \times 74 + 49 \times 74$
$= 74 \times (50 + 49 + 1)$
$= 74 \times 100$
$= 7,400$

(t) $81 + 5 \times 810 + 49 \times 81$
$= 81 + 5 \times 10 \times 81 + 49 \times 81$
$= 81 \times (50 + 49 + 1)$
$= 81 \times 100$
$= 8,100$

Page 111,112

4. (a)
```
    3 4
+ 3 4 0
-------
  3 7 4
```

(b)
```
    4 5
+ 4 5 0
-------
  4 9 5
```

(c)
```
    2 7
+ 2 7 0
-------
  2 9 7
```

(d)
```
    3 7
+ 3 7 0
-------
  4 0 7
```

(e)
```
    3 4 5
+ 3 4 5 0
---------
  3 7 9 5
```

(f)
```
    1 2 3
+ 1 2 3 0
---------
  1 3 5 3
```

(g)
```
    4 2 6
+ 4 2 6 0
---------
  4 6 8 6
```

(h)
```
    2 8 6
+ 2 8 6 0
---------
  3 1 4 6
```

(i) 14×101
$= 1,414$

(j) 67×101
$= 6,767$

(k) 23×101
$= 2,323$

(l) 45×101
$= 4,545$

(m) 82×101
$= 8,282$

(n) 98×101
$= 9,898$

(o) 63×101
$= 6,363$

(p) 76×101
$= 7,676$

Page 113,114

5. (a) $4 \times (4 + 1) = 20$
$3 \times 7 = 21$
$43 \times 47 = 2,021$

(b) $5 \times (5 + 1) = 30$
$4 \times 6 = 24$
$54 \times 56 = 3,024$

(c) $5 \times (5 + 1) = 30$
$2 \times 8 = 16$
$52 \times 58 = 3,016$

(d) $6 \times (6 + 1) = 42$
$6 \times 4 = 24$
$66 \times 64 = 4,224$

(e) $7 \times (7 + 1) = 56$
$3 \times 7 = 21$
$73 \times 77 = 5,621$

(f) $8 \times (8 + 1) = 72$
$9 \times 1 = 9$
$89 \times 81 = 7,209$

(g) $9 \times (9 + 1) = 90$
$2 \times 8 = 16$
$92 \times 98 = 9,016$

(h) $5 \times (5 + 1) = 30$
$7 \times 3 = 21$
$57 \times 53 = 3,021$

(i) $4 \times (4 + 1) = 20$
$2 \times 8 = 16$
$42 \times 48 = 2,016$

(j) $8 \times (8 + 1) = 72$
$5 \times 5 = 25$
$85 \times 85 = 7,225$

(k) $4 \times (4 + 1) = 20$
$4 \times 6 = 24$
$44 \times 46 = 2,024$

(l) $7 \times (7 + 1) = 56$
$4 \times 6 = 24$
$74 \times 76 = 5,624$

318

978-1-62399-074-9
Singapore Math Challenge

Chapter 8 Practice
Page 120
1. Use a table.

	Zachary	Nicholas	Philip
accountant			✗
bus driver	✗	✗	✓
manager			

From the above table, Philip must be the bus driver.
Since Philip is older than the accountant but younger than Nicholas, Nicholas must be the manager. Zachary is the accountant.

Page 121
2. Each reading is the total weight of two girls. If the three readings are added, the total is equivalent to the weight of 6 people.
45 kg + 55 kg + 50 kg = 150 kg
150 kg ÷ 2 = 75 kg
So, the total weight of the three girls is 75 kg.
75 kg – 45 kg = 30 kg
75 kg – 55 kg = 20 kg
75 kg – 50 kg = 25 kg
Sabrina is 30 kg, Kim is 25 kg and Bernice is 20 kg.

Page 122
3. $8 \times \bigcirc = 64$
$\bigcirc = 64 \div 8 = 8$
$\square = 7 \times 8 = 56$
4. $\triangle = 5 \times \bigcirc$
$5 \times \bigcirc \times \bigcirc = 45$
$\bigcirc \times \bigcirc = 45 \div 5 = 9$
$\bigcirc = 3$
$\triangle = 3 \times 5 = 15$

Page 123
5. Use a table.

	Calvin	Leon	Henry
doctor			
teacher	✗	✗	✓
army officer			✗

From the above table, Henry must be the teacher. Since Henry is older than the army officer but younger than Leon, Calvin must be the army officer and Leon must be the doctor.

Page 124
6. Based on the given hints, below is the ranking.
youngest   **oldest**
B   D   C   E   A

Page 125
7. If the 4th witness is telling the truth, it means that the 3rd witness is telling a lie.
So, the testimonies of the first and second witnesses are not reliable. Both suspects A and B are guilty of shoplifting.

Page 126
8. Since all the children are under 9 years old, we assume that the oldest child, Royston, must be 8 years old.
As each family had only one child three years ago, Mr. Wood's and Mr. Smith's younger children must be under 3 years old. So, Mr. Smith's younger child is 1 year old and Mr. Wood's younger child, Jack, is 2 years old.
Sean must be Mr. Smith's child and should be 8 ÷ 2 = 4 years old.
Mike is 4 – 3 = 1 year old.
<u>Mr. Wood's children</u>
Royston (8 years old)
Jack (2 years old)
<u>Mr. Smith's children</u>
Sean (4 years old)
Mike (1 year old)

Page 127

9. If Sean took the chocolate cake,

	Truth	Lie
Sean		✓
Cindy	✓	
Jack	✓	

If Cindy took the chocolate cake,

	Truth	Lie
Sean	✓	
Cindy		✓
Jack		✓

If Jack took the chocolate cake,

	Truth	Lie
Sean	✓	
Cindy	✓	
Jack		✓

Since one of them was telling the truth, Cindy must be the one who took the chocolate cake.

Page 128

10. $\square + \square + \ast + \ast + \clubsuit + \clubsuit = 11 + 9 + 10$
$$= 30$$

$\square + \ast + \clubsuit = 30 \div 2$
$$= 15$$

So:
$$\clubsuit = 15 - 11 = 4$$
$$\ast = 15 - 9 = 6$$
$$\square = 15 - 10 = 5$$

11. $\bigcirc + \bigcirc + \triangle + \triangle + \clubsuit + \clubsuit = 22 + 18 + 20$
$$= 60$$

$\bigcirc + \triangle + \clubsuit = 60 \div 2$
$$= 30$$

So:
$$\clubsuit = 30 - 22 = 8$$
$$\triangle = 30 - 18 = 12$$
$$\bigcirc = 30 - 20 = 10$$

Page 129

12.

	A	B	C	D	E	F	G	H
first meeting	✓	✓	✓	✓				
second meeting		✓			✓	✓	✓	
third meeting	✓	✓			✓		✓	

From the above table, B attended all the meetings and H did not attend any. So, B and H are from the same class. C and E are from the same class. A and F are from the same class. D and G are from the same class.

Page 130

13. If Jacelyn took the blueberry pie,

	Truth	Lie
Jacelyn		✓
Kate	✓	
Polly	✓	

If Kate took the blueberry pie,

	Truth	Lie
Jacelyn	✓	
Kate		✓
Polly	✓	

If Polly took the blueberry pie,

	Truth	Lie
Jacelyn		✓
Kate	✓	
Polly		✓

Since only one kid was telling the truth, Polly must be the one who took half of the blueberry pie.

Page 131

14. □ + ❖ = 50 − 36 = 14
□ + □ + ❖ + ❖ + ❖ = 36
14 + 14 + ❖ = 36
❖ = 36 − 14 − 14 = 8
□ = 14 − 8 = 6

15. ○ + □ = 55 − 43 = 12
○ + ○ + ○ + □ + □ + □ + □ = 43
12 + 12 + 12 + □ = 43
□ = 43 − 12 − 12 − 12 = 7
○ = 12 − 7
   = 5

Page 132

16. There are 31 days in January and 7 days in a week.
31 ÷ 7 = 4 R 3
This means that 4 days of the week will appear 4 times and the remaining 3 days of the week will appear 5 times in the month of January.
So, the 4 days should be Friday, Saturday, Sunday and Monday. Therefore, the 1st of January in that year was on Tuesday.
We can use the table below for checking.

Sun.	Mon.	Tues.	Wed.	Thurs.	Fri.	Sat.
		1	2	3	4	5
6	7	8	9	10	11	12
13	14	15	16	17	18	19
20	21	22	23	24	25	26
27	28	29	30	31		

Page 133

17. If Sean is lying, Karen could be the tallest among them.
If Karen is lying, she or Kelvin could be the shortest. This should not be the case.
If Susan is lying, she or Kelvin could be the shortest. This should not be the case.
If Kelvin is lying, no one is the shortest. This should not be the case.
So, Sean must be lying.

tallest			**shortest**
Karen	Sean	Susan	Kelvin

Page 134

18. Use a drawing.

In this drawing, Team C has played one game.

Page 135

19. If Bob broke the window,

	Truth	Lie
Bob		✓
Katy	✓	
Joe	✓	

If Katy broke the window,

	Truth	Lie
Bob		✓
Katy		✓
Joe	✓	

If Joe broke the window,

	Truth	Lie
Bob	✓	
Katy	✓	
Joe		✓

Since only one child was telling the truth, Katy must be the one who broke the window.

978-1-62399-074-9
Singapore Math Challenge

Page 136

20. If Joshua flew the paper airplane,

	Truth	Lie
Joshua		✓
Paul	✓	
James	✓	

If Paul flew the paper airplane,

	Truth	Lie
Joshua	✓	
Paul		✓
James		✓

If James flew the paper airplane,

	Truth	Lie
Joshua	✓	
Paul	✓	
James		✓

Since only one of them was telling the truth, Paul must be the one who flew the paper airplane.

Page 137

21.

	French	American	Russian	Romanian
Number 22	✓		✗	
Number 23		✗		✓
Number 24		✓		
Number 24			✓	✗

The number tags of the French, American, Russian and Romanian runners are 22, 24, 25 and 23 respectively.

Page 138

22. There are 31 days in March and 7 days in a week.

$31 \div 7 = 4\,R\,3$

This means that 4 days of the week will appear 4 times and the remaining 3 days of the week will appear 5 times in the month of March.

So, the 4 days should be Wednesday, Thursday, Friday and Saturday.

Use the table below to find the day of March 10th.

Sun.	Mon.	Tues.	Wed.	Thurs.	Fri.	Sat.
1	2	3	4	5	6	7
8	9	10	11	12	13	14
15	16	17	18	19	20	21
22	23	24	25	26	27	28
29	30	31				

The 10th of March in that year was on Tuesday.

978-1-62399-074-9
Singapore Math Challenge

Chapter 9 Practice

Page 142

1. 900 m ÷ 150 m = 6 min.
   It takes 6 minutes for him to run a distance of 900 meters.

2. Distance = Speed × Time
   $\qquad\quad$ = 120 m/min. × 5 min.
   $\qquad\quad$ = 600 m
   She can bike 600 meters in 5 minutes.

Page 143

3. 12 sec. → 60 m
   $\quad$ 1 sec. → 60 ÷ 12 = 5 m
   400 m ÷ 5 m = 80 sec.
   He takes 80 seconds to jog 400 meters.

4. 5 min. → 800 m
   1 min. → 800 ÷ 5 = 160 m
   1,280 m ÷ 160 m = 8 min.
   It takes 8 minutes for him to cover a distance of 1,280 meters.

Page 144

5. $\qquad\quad$ 60 sec. → 50 m
   4 × 60 = 240 sec. → 4 × 50 = 200 m
   He can cover 200 meters in 240 seconds.

6. 80 m – 70 m = 10 m
   Elaine was behind Diana by 10 m every minute.
   1 min. → 10 m
   8 min. → 8 × 10 m = 80 m
   Elaine was 80 meters behind Diana after 8 minutes.

Page 145

7. 200 m – 180 m = 20 m
   Joe was 20 m ahead of his brother every minute.
   1 min. → 20 m
   10 min. → 20 × 10 = 200 m
   Joe was 200 meters ahead of his brother after 10 minutes.

8. 4 m – 2 m = 2 m
   The cat could run 2 m faster than the rat every second.
   1 sec. → 2 m
   20 m ÷ 2 m = 10 sec.
   The cat would take 10 seconds to catch the rat.

Page 146

9. 12 m – 7 m = 5 m
   The hound can run 5 m faster than the rabbit every second.
   1 sec. → 5 m
   50 m ÷ 5 m = 10 sec.
   The hound takes 10 seconds to catch up with the rabbit.

10. 15 m – 10 m = 5 m
    The jaguar could run 5 m faster than its prey every second.
    1 sec. → 5 m
    100 m ÷ 5 m = 20 sec.
    The jaguar would take 20 seconds to catch its prey.

Page 147

11. *Method 1: Make A List*

Time	Distance by Mr. Thomas	Distance by Jacklyn	Distance between them
5th min.	200 m/min. × 5 min. = 1,000 m	0 m	1,000 m – 0 m = 1,000 m
6th min.	1,200 m	400 m/min. × 1 min. = 400 m	1,200 m – 400 m = 800 m
7th min.	1,400 m	800 m	1,400 m – 800 m = 600 m
8th min.	1,600 m	1,200 m	1,600 m – 1,200 m = 400 m
9th min.	1,800 m	1,600 m	1,800 m – 1,600 m = 200 m
10th min.	2,000 m	2,000 m	2,000 m – 2,000 m = 0 m

10 – 5 = 5

Method 2: Solve By Reasoning
400 m/min. – 200 m/min. = 200 m/min.
Jacklyn's biking speed was 200 m/min. faster than her dad's jogging speed.
200 m/min. × 5 min. = 1,000 m
Mr. Thomas had jogged 1,000 m before Jacklyn started to bike.
Time Jacklyn took to catch up
= Difference in distance ÷ Difference in speed
= 1,000 m ÷ 200 m/min.
= 5 min.
Jacklyn would take 5 minutes to catch up with her dad.

Page 148

12. *Method 1: Make A List*

Time	Distance traveled by the first train	Distance traveled by the express train	Distance between the two trains
5th hour	6 km/h × 5 hours = 300 km	0 km	300 km – 0 km = 300 km
6th hour	360 km	120 km/h × 1 hour = 120 km	360 km – 120 km = 240 km
7th hour	420 km	240 km	420 km – 240 km = 180 km
8th hour	480 km	360 km	480 km – 360 km = 120 km
9th hour	540 km	480 km	540 km – 480 km = 60 km
10th hour	600 km	600 km	600 km – 600 km = 0 km

10 – 5 = 5

Method 2: Solve By Reasoning

120 km/h – 60 km/h = 60 km/h

The express train was 60 km/h faster than that of the first train.

60 km/h × 5 hours = 300 km

The first train had traveled 300 km before the express train started its journey.

Time that the express train took to catch up
= Difference in distance ÷ Difference in speed
= 300 km ÷ 60 km/h
= 5 hours

The express train took 5 hours to catch up with the first train.

Page 149

13. Time = Distance ÷ Speed
    = 560 km ÷ 70 km/h
    = 8 hours

8 hours – 1 hour = 7 hours

Speed = Distance ÷ Time
    = 560 km ÷ 7 hours
    = 80 km/h

Sam should drive at 80 km/h if he wants to arrive at the destination an hour early.

80 km/h – 70 km/h = 10 km/h

Sam should increase his driving speed by 10 km/h.

14. From 9 am to 3 pm, it is 6 hours.

50 km/h × 6 hours = 300 km

The distance to Town B was 300 km.

From 10 am to 3 pm, it is 5 hours.

Speed = Distance ÷ Time
    = 300 km ÷ 5 hours
    = 60 km/h

The speed that the train had to travel in order to arrive in Town B at 3 pm was 60 km/h.

Page 150

15. There are 8 hours from 8 am to 4 pm.

60 km/h × 8 hours = 480 km

Instead of 8 hours, the train took 10 hours to travel 480 km.

Speed = Distance ÷ Time
    = 480 km ÷ 10 hours
    = 48 km/h

Its actual speed for the journey would be 48 km/h.

16. 40 m/min. × 10 min. = 400 m
The school was 400 m away from Cindy's house.
From 7:04 am to 7:12 am, it is 8 minutes.
So, Cindy had to cover a distance of 400 m in 8 min.
Speed = Distance ÷ Time
= 400 m ÷ 8 min.
= 50 m/min.
She walked at a speed of 50 m/min.

Page 151

17. (a) Time = Distance ÷ Speed
= 300 m ÷ 50 m/min.
= 6 min.
Samuel takes 6 minutes to walk to school.
Time = Distance ÷ Speed
= 300 m ÷ 60 m/min.
= 5 min.
John takes 5 minutes to walk to school.
(b) 7:00 + 6 = 7:06
Samuel will reach the school at 7:06 am.
7:01 + 5 = 7:06
John will reach the school at 7:06 am.

18. *Method 1: Make A Table*

Time	Distance that Alex has run	Distance that William has run
1st	0 m	320 m/min. × 1 min. = 320 m
2nd	400 m/min. × 1 min. = 400 m	640 m
3rd	800 m	960 m
4th	1,200 m	1,280 m
5th	1,600 m	1,600 m

Method 2: Solve By Reasoning
William is 320 m ahead.
The difference in speed = 400 – 320
= 80 m/min.
That is how fast Alex can catch up, 80 m in one minute.
320 m ÷ 80 m/min. = 4 min.
4 + 1 = 5
William has been running for 5 minutes when Alex catches up with him.

Page 152

19. 50 m/min. × 5 min. = 250 m
John has to walk another 250 m when the bell rings.
70 m/sec. × 5 min. = 350 m
The distance John can continue to cover before the bell rings is 350 m.
250 m + 350 m = 600 m
The difference in the distance when John walks at 50 m/min. and 70 m/min. respectively is 600 m.
70 m/min. – 50 m/min. = 20 m/min.
600 m ÷ 20 m/min. = 30 min.
John takes 30 min. to walk to school.
50 m/min. × 30 min. = 1,500 m
1,500 m + 250 m = 1,750 m
      OR
70 m/min. × 30 min. = 2,100 m
2,100 m – 350 m = 1,750 m
The school is 1,750 m away from John's house.

20. 60 m/min. × 4 min. = 240 m
Alice has to walk another 240 m when the bell rings.
80 m/sec. × 4 min. = 320 m
The distance Alice can continue to cover before the bell rings is 320 m
240 m + 320 m = 560 m
The difference in the distance when Alice walks at 60 m/min. and 80 m/min. respectively is 560 m.
80 m/min. – 60 m/min. = 20 m/min.
560 m ÷ 20 m/min. = 28 min.
Alice takes 28 min. to walk to school.
60 m/min. × 28 min. = 1,680 m
1,680 m + 240 m = 1,920 m
      OR
80 m/min. × 28 min. = 2,240 m
2,240 m – 320 m = 1,920 m
The school is 1,920 m away from Alice's house.

Chapter 10 Practice

Page 156

1.

Natalie   ? m   Her sister
40 m/min.   50 m/min.
              500 m

40 m/min. × 5 min. = 200 m
Natalie walked 200 m in 5 minutes.
50 m/min. × 5 min. = 250 m
Her sister walked 250 m in 5 minutes.
200 m + 250 m = 450 m
500 m – 450 m = 50 m
They were 50 m apart after 5 minutes.

2. 220 m/min. × 5 min. = 1,100 m
Travis biked 1,100 m in 5 minutes.
240 m/min. × 5 min. = 1,200 m
Zane biked 1,200 m in 5 minutes.
2,500 m – 1,100 m – 1,200 m = 200 m
They were 200 m apart after 5 minutes.

Page 157

3. 60 m/min. × 4 min. = 240 m
Adeline can walk 240 m in 4 minutes.
60 m/min. – 10 m/min. = 50 m/min.
50 m/min. × 4 min. = 200 m
Beatrice can walk 200 m in 4 minutes.
500 – 240 – 200 = 60 m
They are 60 m away from each other after 4 minutes.

4. 40 m/min. × 4 min. = 160 m
Sean walked 160 m in 4 minutes.
50 m/min. × 4 min. = 200 m
Richard walked 200 m in 4 minutes.
160 m + 200 m = 360 m
They were 360 m away from each other after 4 minutes.

Page 158

5. 250 m/min. × 4 min. = 1,000 m
John biked 1,000 m in 4 minutes.
300 m/min. × 4 min. = 1,200 m
Mark biked 1,200 m in 4 minutes.
1,000 m + 1,200 m = 2,200 m
They were 2,200 m apart after 4 minutes.

6. (65 km/h × 8 hours) + (60 km/h × 8 hours)
520 km + 480 km = 1,000 km
Town B was 1,000 km from Town A.

Page 159

7. 70 km + 60 km = 130 km
The total distance traveled by the car and the van in an hour is 130 km.
Time = Distance ÷ Speed
      = 390 km ÷ 130 km
      = 3 hours
The car and the van pass each other 3 hours later.
70 km/h × 3 hours = 210 km
The car and the van pass each other at 210 km away from Town X.
        OR
60 km/h × 3 hours = 180 km
The car and the van pass each other at 180 km away from Town Y.

8. 36 km/h + 64 km/h = 100 km/h
The two trains traveled at a total speed of 100 km/h.
Time = Distance ÷ Speed
     = 900 km ÷ 100 km/h
     = 9 hours
The two trains met 9 hours later.

Page 160

9. Speed = Distance ÷ Time
       = 2,000 km ÷ 10 hours
       = 200 km/h
The total speed of cars A and B was 200 km/h.
Since car A was 20 km/h faster than car B,
200 km/h – 20 km/h = 180 km/h
180 km/h ÷ 2 = 90 km/h
The driving speed of car B was 90 km/h.
90 km/h + 20 km/h = 110 km/h
The driving speed of car A was 110 km/h.

10. 50 km/h × 10 hours = 500 km
The faster van travels 500 km.
980 km – 500 km = 480 km
480 km ÷ 10 hours = 48 km/h
The speed of the slower van is 48 km/h.

Page 161

11. 10 min. – 5 min. = 5 min.
Charles biked for 5 min. before meeting Sean.
220 m/min. × 5 min. = 1,100 m
Charles biked a distance of 1,100 m before meeting Sean.
1,600 m – 1,100 m = 500 m
500 m ÷ 10 min. = 50 m/min.
Sean's walking speed was 50 m/min.

12. *Method 1: Make A List*

Time	Distance by car A	Distance by car B	Total distance
1st hour	32 km/h × 1 h = 32 km	0 km	32 km + 0 km = 32 km
2nd hour	64 km	64 km/h × 1 hour = 64 km	64 km + 64 km = 128 km
3rd hour	96 km	128 km	96 km + 128 km = 224 km
4th hour	128 km	192 km	128 km + 192 km = 320 km
5th hour	160 km	256 km	160 km + 256 km = 416 km
6th hour	192 km	320 km	192 km + 320 km = 512 km

6 – 1 = 5

Method 2: Solve By Reasoning
512 km – 32 km = 480 km
The distance between the two cars was 480 km after car A had traveled for an hour.
32 km/h × 2 = 64 km/h
Car B's speed was 64 km/h.
32 km/h + 64 km/h = 96 km/h
The total speed of cars A and B in an hour was 96 km/h.
480 km ÷ 96 km/h = 5 hours
It would take 5 hours for the two cars to pass each other after car B left Town Z.

978-1-62399-074-9
Singapore Math Challenge

Page 162

13. 30 m/min. + 40 m/min. = 70 m/min.
Our total walking speed was 70 m/min.
Time = Distance ÷ Speed
       = 700 m ÷ 70 m/min.
       = 10 min.
I would meet my brother 10 minutes later.
40 m/min. × 10 min. = 400 m
I would meet my brother 400 m away from my house.

14. Time = Distance ÷ Speed
       = 250 m ÷ 50 m/min.
       = 5 min.
It took 5 min. for me to meet my brother on the way.
60 m/min. × 5 min. = 300 m
My brother had walked 300 m before we met.
250 m + 300 m = 550 m
The shopping mall was 550 m from my house.

Page 163

15. 60 km/h + 20 km/h = 80 km/h
The speed of Train B was 80 km/h.
60 km + 80 km = 140 km
Trains A and B traveled 140 km in an hour.
140 km/h × 6 hours = 840 km
Town D was 840 km from Town C.

16. Time = Distance ÷ Speed
       = 100 m ÷ 20 m/min.
       = 5 min.
Charles had walked for 5 min. before he met Jonathan. Jonathan walked for 5 min. too.
30 m/min. × 5 min. = 150 m
100 m + 150 m = 250 m
Jonathan's house was 250 m from Charles's.

Page 164

17. Time = Distance ÷ Speed
       = 350 m ÷ 70 km/h
       = 5 hours
The first car had traveled for 5 hours before the two cars passed each other. The second car traveled for 5 hours too.
80 km/h × 5 hours = 400 km
350 km + 400 km = 750 km
Valley Town was 750 km from Richmond Town.

18.

100 m + 500 m = 600 m
The train travels a total of 600 m.
Time = Distance ÷ Speed
       = 600 m ÷ 20 m/sec.
       = 30 sec.
It will take 30 seconds to cross a bridge of 500 m long.

978-1-62399-074-9
Singapore Math Challenge

Page 165

19.

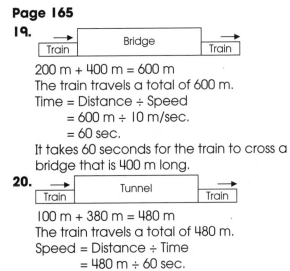

200 m + 400 m = 600 m
The train travels a total of 600 m.
Time = Distance ÷ Speed
   = 600 m ÷ 10 m/sec.
   = 60 sec.
It takes 60 seconds for the train to cross a bridge that is 400 m long.

20.

100 m + 380 m = 480 m
The train travels a total of 480 m.
Speed = Distance ÷ Time
   = 480 m ÷ 60 sec.
   = 8 m/sec.
The train is traveling at 8 m/sec.

Chapter 11 Practice

Page 173

1.   44 – 4 = 40
     Isabelle's mother was 40 years old four years ago.
     40 ÷ 4 = 10
     Isabelle was 10 years old four years ago.
     10 + 4 = 14
     Isabelle is 14 years old.

Page 174

2.   *Method 1: Solve Using a Model*
     34 – 8 = 26
     The age difference is 26 years.
     26 ÷ 2 = 13
     13 × 3 = 39
     His mother is 39 years old when her age is three times Joel's age.

     Method 2: Make a List

His mother's age	Joel's age	Difference	Was his mother's age three times Joel's age?
34	8	26	No
36	10	26	No
38	12	26	No
39	13	26	Yes

     39 – 34 = 5   or   13 – 8 = 5
     His mother's age will be three times Joel's age in 5 years' time.

Page 175

3.   *Method 1: Solve Using a Model*
     34 – 10 = 24 (their age difference)
     24 ÷ 3 = 8
     8 × 4 = 32
     Her father was 32 years old when his age was four times Beatrice's age.
     34 – 32 = 2

     Method 2: Make a List

Father's age	Beatrice's age	Difference	Was her father's age four times Beatrice's age?
34	10	24	No
33	9	24	No
32	8	24	Yes

     34 – 32 = 2   or   10 – 8 = 2
     Her father's age was four times Beatrice's age 2 years ago.

329

Page 176

4. $66 + 3 + 3 = 72$

Three years later, the sum of their ages will be 72 years.

$72 \div 9 = 8$

$8 - 3 = 5$

Jimmy is 5 years old now.

$8 \times 8 = 64$

$64 - 3 = 61$

His grandfather is 61 years old now.

Page 177

5. $64 - 13 = 51$ (their age difference)

Grandmother

Samuel $\quad 64 - 13$

$51 \div 3 = 17$

$17 \times 4 = 68$

Samuel's grandmother will be 68 years old when her age is four times Samuel's age.

$68 - 64 = 4$

His grandmother's age will be four times Samuel's age in 4 years' time.

Page 178

6. *Method 1: Solve Using a Model*

$38 - 8 = 30$ (their age difference)

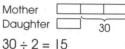

Mother

Daughter $\quad 30$

$30 \div 2 = 15$

$15 \times 3 = 45$

The mother will be 45 years old when her age is three times the daughter's age.

$45 - 38 = 7$

Method 2: Make a List

Mother's age	Daughter's age	Difference	Is one 3 times the other?
38	8	30	No
40	10	30	No, 4 times
42	12	30	No
44	14	30	No
45	15	30	Yes

$45 - 38 = 7$ or $15 - 8 = 7$

The mother will be three times the daughter's age in 7 years' time.

Page 179

7. $35 - 5 = 30$

$30 \div 2 = 15$

Her brother is 15 years old.

$15 + 5 = 20$

Melanie is 20 years old.

8. $14 - 10 = 4$

Their age difference is 4 years.

$50 - 4 = 46$

$46 \div 2 = 23$

Jonathan will be 23 years old.

$23 + 4 = 27$

Joseph will be 27 years old.

Page 180

9. *Method 1: Solve Using a Model*

60 – 5 = 55 (their age difference)

Granny Mabel

Kelly   55

55 ÷ 5 = 11

11 × 6 = 66

Granny Mabel will be 66 years old when her age is six times Kelly's age.

66 – 60 = 6

Method 2: Make a List

Granny Mabel's age	Kelly's age	Difference	Was Granny Mabel's age six times Kelly's age?
60	5	55	No
62	7	55	No
64	9	55	No
65	10	55	No
66	11	55	Yes

66 – 60 = 6   or   11 – 5 = 6

Granny Mabel's age will be six times Kelly's age in 6 years' time.

Page 181

10. *Method 1: Solve Using a Model*

50 – 24 = 26 (their age difference)

Father

Son   26

26 ÷ 2 = 13

13 × 3 = 39

The father was 39 years old when his age was three times his son's age.

50 – 39 = 11

Method 2: Make a List

Father's age	Son's age	Difference	Was the father's age three times his son's age?
50	24	26	No
46	20	26	No
40	14	26	No
39	13	26	Yes

50 – 39 = 11   or   24 – 13 = 11

The father's age was three times his son's age 11 years ago.

Page 182

11.

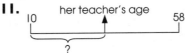

The number of years it takes for Jenevieve to be as old as her teacher is the same as the number of years it takes for her teacher to be 58 years old.

58 – 10 = 48

48 ÷ 2 = 24

24 + 10 = 34

Her teacher is 34 years old.

12.

Auntie Zoe's age

12   62

?

The number of years it takes for Cindy to be as old as Auntie Zoe is the same as the number of years it takes for Auntie Zoe to be 62 years old.

62 – 12 = 50

50 ÷ 2 = 25

25 + 12 = 37

Auntie Zoe is 37 years old.

Page 183

13. $60 - 8 - 8 = 44$

Eight years ago, the sum of the father's and his son's age was 44 years.

$44 \div 4 = 11$

$11 \times 3 = 33$

The father and his son were 33 and 11 years old respectively eight years ago.

$11 + 8 = 19$

$33 + 8 = 41$

The father and his son are now 41 and 19 years old respectively.

14. $50 + 5 + 5 = 60$

The sum of the father's and his daughter's ages will be 60 years five years from now.

$60 \div 4 = 15$

$15 \times 3 = 45$

The father and his daughter will be 45 and 15 years old respectively five years from now.

$45 - 5 = 40$

$15 - 5 = 10$

The father is 40 years old and his daughter is 10 years old.

Page 184

15. The difference in their age is 30 years.

Mother [   ][   ][   ][   ]

David [   ]   30

$30 \div 3 = 10$

$10 - 8 = 2$

David is 2 years old now.

16. The difference in their age is 50 years.

Grandfather [   ][   ][   ][   ][   ][   ]

Raymond [   ]   50

$50 \div 5 = 10$

$10 \times 6 = 60$

$60 + 6 = 66$

Raymond's grandfather is 66 years old now.

Chapter 12 Practice

Page 192

1.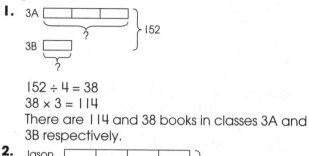

$152 \div 4 = 38$

$38 \times 3 = 114$

There are 114 and 38 books in classes 3A and 3B respectively.

2.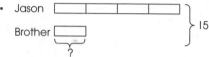

$15 \div 5 = 3$

His brother is 3 years old.

Page 193

3. father [   ][   ][   ][   ]

Valerie [   ] $\Big\}$ 50

$50 \div 5 = 10$

Valerie is 10 years old.

4. chickens [   ][   ][   ][   ]

rabbits [   ] $\Big\}$ 35

$35 \div 5 = 7$

$7 \times 4 = 28$

The number of chickens on the farm is 28 and the number of rabbits is 7.

Page 194

5.

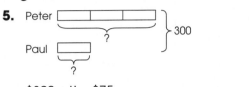

$300 \div 4 = \$75$
$\$75 \times 3 = \$225$
Paul received $75 and Peter received $225.

6. peach trees, apple trees, 120

$120 - 20 = 100$
$100 \div 2 = 50$
There are 50 apples trees in the orchard.

Page 195

7. Valerie, 6, 60, John

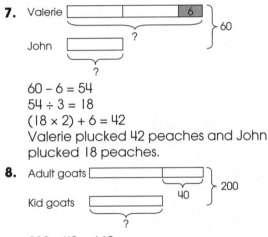

$60 - 6 = 54$
$54 \div 3 = 18$
$(18 \times 2) + 6 = 42$
Valerie plucked 42 peaches and John plucked 18 peaches.

8. Adult goats, Kid goats, 40, 200

$200 - 40 = 160$
$160 \div 2 = 80$
80 kid goats are on the farm.

Page 196

9. Brother, Melvin, 45 + 75

$45 + 75 = 120$
There are a total of 120 storybooks.
$120 \div 4 = 30$
$30 \times 3 = 90$
His brother will have 90 storybooks in the end.
$45 - 30 = 15$ or $90 - 75 = 15$
Melvin must give his brother 15 storybooks
so that his brother has three times as many
storybooks as Melvin.

10. Calvin, Jay, 30 + 45

$30 + 45 = 75$
There are a total of 75 colorful erasers.
$75 \div 3 = 25$
Jay has 25 colorful erasers in the end.
$25 \times 2 = 50$
Calvin has 50 colorful erasers in the end.
$45 - 25 = 20$ or $50 - 30 = 20$
Jay must give Calvin 20 colorful erasers.

Page 197

11. Farm B, Farm A, 300 + 250

$300 + 250 = 550$
There are a total of 550 cows.
$550 \div 5 = 110$
There will be 110 cows on Farm A in the end.
$110 \times 4 = 440$
There will be 440 cows on Farm B in the end.
$300 - 110 = 190$ or $440 - 250 = 190$
190 cows from Farm A must be transferred
to Farm B.

12.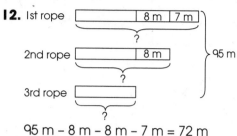

95 m − 8 m − 8 m − 7 m = 72 m
72 m ÷ 3 = 24 m
The length of the third rope is 24 m.
24 m + 8 m = 32 m
The length of the second rope is 32 m.
32 m + 7 m = 39 m
The length of the first rope is 39 m.

Page 198

13.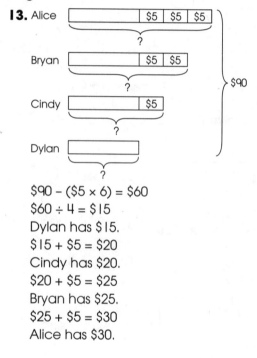

$90 − ($5 × 6) = $60
$60 ÷ 4 = $15
Dylan has $15.
$15 + $5 = $20
Cindy has $20.
$20 + $5 = $25
Bryan has $25.
$25 + $5 = $30
Alice has $30.

14.

A [8ℓ | 2ℓ]
?
B [8ℓ] ⎫ 54ℓ
?
C [ ]
?

54 ℓ − 8 ℓ − 8 ℓ − 2 ℓ = 36 ℓ
36 ℓ ÷ 3 = 12 ℓ
Container C contains 12 ℓ of water.
12 ℓ + 8 ℓ = 20 ℓ
Container B contains 20 ℓ of water.
20 ℓ + 2 ℓ = 22 ℓ
Container A contains 22 ℓ of water.

Page 199

15.

John [ ]
?
Sean [|] ⎫ $1,160
?
Andy [ ]
?

$1,160 ÷ 4 = $290
John and Andy each save $290.
$290 × 2 = $580
Sean saves $580.

16.

1st shelf [20]
?
2nd shelf [20 | 17] ⎫ 270
?
3rd shelf [17]
?

270 ÷ 3 = 90
There are 90 books on each shelf of the bookcase in the end.
90 + 20 = 110
There are 110 books on the first shelf of the bookcase at first.
90 − 20 − 17 = 53
There are 53 books on the second shelf of the bookcase at first.
90 + 17 = 107
There are 107 books on the third shelf of the bookcase at first.

Page 200

17.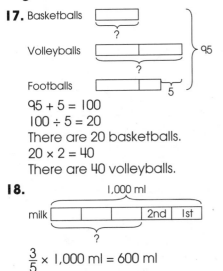

95 + 5 = 100
100 ÷ 5 = 20
There are 20 basketballs.
20 × 2 = 40
There are 40 volleyballs.

18.

milk

$\frac{3}{5}$ × 1,000 ml = 600 ml
600 ml of milk was left.

Page 201

19. pizza [| | | B | S | J]
From the above model,
$\frac{3}{6}$ or $\frac{1}{2}$ of the pizza was left.

20.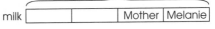

$\frac{2}{4}$ × 1,000 ml = 500 ml
500 ml of the milk was left.

Page 202

21.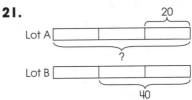

3 × 20 = 60
60 cars were in parking lot A at first.

22.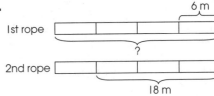

4 × 6 m = 24 m
Each rope is 24 m long at first.

Page 203

23.

Yvonne [| | | |] $11
Vicky [| | |] $44

$11 × 10 = $110
They have $110 altogether at first.

24.

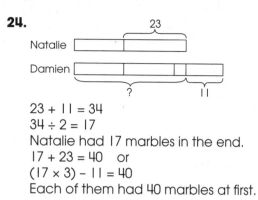

23 + 11 = 34
34 ÷ 2 = 17
Natalie had 17 marbles in the end.
17 + 23 = 40   or
(17 × 3) – 11 = 40
Each of them had 40 marbles at first.

Page 204

25.

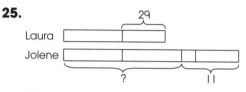

29 + 33 = 62
62 ÷ 2 = 31
Laura had 31 marbles in the end.
31 + 29 = 60   or
(31 × 3) – 33 = 60
Each of them have 60 marbles at first.

26.

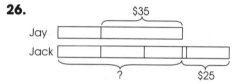

$35 + $25 = $60
$60 ÷ 3 = $20
Jay had $20 in the end.
$20 + $35 = $55   or
($20 × 4) – $25 = $55
Each of them had $55 at first.

Chapter 13 Practice

Page 210

1. 4 apples + 3 peaches → $10
4 apples + 6 peaches → $16
By comparison,
6 peaches – 3 peaches → $16 – $10
3 peaches → $6
1 peach   → $6 ÷ 3 = $2
The cost of each peach is $2.

2. 6 color ink + 3 black ink → $150
6 color ink + 5 black ink → $170
By comparison,
5 black ink – 3 black ink → $170 – $150
2 black ink → $20
1 black ink → $20 ÷ 2 = $10
6 color ink + (3 black ink × $10) → $150
6 color ink → $150 – $30 = $120
1 color ink → $120 ÷ 6 = $20
The cost of each color ink cartridge is $20.

Page 211

3. 3 chocolate bars + 4 packets of candy
→ 200 g
3 chocolate bars + 7 packets of candy
→ 260 g
By comparison,
7 packets –4 packets → 260 g – 200 g
3 packets → 60 g
1 packet   → 60 g ÷ 3 = 20 g
3 chocolate bars + (4 packets × 20 g) → 200 g
3 chocolate bars → 200 g – 80 g = 120 g
1 chocolate bar → 120 g ÷ 3 = 40 g
The weight of a chocolate bar is 40 g.

4. 3 boxes of apples + 5 boxes of oranges
→ 270 kg
3 boxes of apples + 7 boxes of oranges
→ 342 kg
By comparison,
7 boxes of oranges – 5 boxes of oranges
→ 342 kg – 270 kg
2 boxes of oranges → 72 kg
1 box of oranges   → 36 kg
3 boxes of apples + (5 boxes of oranges × 36 kg)
→ 270 kg
3 boxes of apples → 270 – 180 = 90 kg
1 box of apples   → 90 kg ÷ 3 = 30 kg
A box of apples weighs 30 kg and a box of
oranges weighs 36 kg.

Page 212

5. 4 jugs + 5 cups → $85
2 jugs + 2 cups → $40
To make the two mathematical statements comparable, multiply the second statement by 2.
 4 jugs + 4 cups → $80
 5 cups – 4 cups → $85 – $80
   1 cup → $5
The cost of a cup is $5.

6. 4 apples + 3 peaches → $10
2 apples + 2 peaches → $6
To make the two mathematical statements comparable, multiply the second statement by 2.
4 apples + 4 peaches → $6 × 2 = $12
4 peaches – 3 peaches → $12 – $10
1 peach → $2
2 apples + (2 peaches × $2) → $6
2 apples → $6 – $4 = $2
1 apple → $2 ÷ 2 = $1
The cost of an apple is $1.

Page 213

7. 5 basketballs + 6 volleyballs → $320
2 basketballs + 3 volleyballs → $140
To make the two mathematical statements comparable, multiply the second statement by 2.
4 basketballs + 6 voleyballs → $280
5 basketballs – 4 basketballs → $320 – $280
              = $40
1 basketball → $40
The cost of a basketball is $40.

8. 3 big pails + 4 small pails → 68 ℓ
4 big pails + 2 small pails → 64 ℓ
To make the two mathematical statements comparable, multiply the second statement by 2.
8 big pails + 4 small pails → 128 ℓ
8 big pails – 3 big pails → 128 ℓ – 68 ℓ = 60 ℓ
5 big pails → 60 ℓ
1 big pail → 60 ℓ ÷ 5 = 12 ℓ
A big pail can hold 12 ℓ of water.

Page 214

9. 1 table + 3 chairs → $120
Since the table costs 3 times as much as each chair,
1 table = 3 chairs
Replace the table in the first statement by 3 chairs.
3 chairs + 3 chairs → $120
        6 chairs → $120
        3 chairs → $120 ÷ 2 = $60
The cost of the table is $60.

10. 2 scooters + 3 bicycles → $560
Since each scooter costs twice as much as each bicycle,
2 scooters = 4 bicycles
4 bicycles + 3 bicycles → $560
7 bicycles → $560
1 bicycle → $560 ÷ 7 = $80
2 × $80 = $160
The cost of each scooter is $160.

978-1-62399-074-9
Singapore Math Challenge

Page 215

11. 4 tables + 9 chairs → $504

Since the cost of each table was the cost of 3 such chairs,

1 table = 3 chairs

4 tables = 12 chairs

12 chairs + 9 chairs → $504

21 chairs → $504

1 chair → $504 ÷ 21 = $24

The cost of each chair was $24.

12. 4 basketballs + 5 volleyballs → $330

Since the price of 2 basketballs is the same as the price of 3 volleyballs,

2 basketballs = 3 volleyballs

(2 × 2 = 4) basketballs = (3 × 2 = 6) volleyballs

6 volleyballs + 5 volleyballs → $330

11 volleyballs → $330

1 volleyball → $330 ÷ 11 = $30

The price of a volleyball was $30.

Page 216

13. 4 basketballs + 5 volleyballs → $520

5 basketballs + 4 volleyballs → $533

$533 – $520 = $13

(difference of one basketball and one volleyball)

4 basketballs = 4 volleyballs + (4 × $13)

= 4 volleyballs + $52

4 volleyballs + $52 + 5 volleyballs → $520

9 volleyballs → $520 – $52 = $468

1 volleyball → $468 ÷ 9 = $52

1 basketball → $52 + $13 = $65

Each volleyball was $52 and each basketball was $65.

14. Let the number of white, red and black balls be w, r and b respectively.

$w + r = 15$

$r + b = 18$

$b + w = 9$

$(2 × w) + (2 × r) + (2 × b) = 15 + 18 + 9$

$= 42$

$w + r + b = 42 ÷ 2 = 21$

$b = 21 – 15 = 6$

$w = 21 – 18 = 3$

$r = 21 – 9 = 12$

There are 6 black balls, 3 white balls and 12 red balls.

Page 217

15. Let the number of red, yellow and oranges roses be r, y and o respectively.

$r + y = 60$

$y + o = 70$

$o + r = 80$

$(2 × r) + (2 × y) + (2 × o) = 60 + 70 + 80$

$= 210$

$r + y + o = 210 ÷ 2 = 105$

$o = 105 – 60 = 45$

$r = 105 – 70 = 35$

$y = 105 – 80 = 25$

The florist sells 45 orange roses, 35 red roses and 25 yellow roses.

16. Let the number of adults, boys and girls be a, b and g respectively.

$a + b = 87$

$a + g = 83$

$b + g = 60$

$(2 × a) + (2 × b) + (2 × g) = 87 + 83 + 60$

$= 230$

$a + b + g = 230 ÷ 2 = 115$

$g = 115 – 87 = 28$

$b = 115 – 83 = 32$

$a = 115 – 60 = 55$

28 girls, 32 boys and 55 adults are at the party.

Page 218

17. Let the number of yellow, blue and red beads be y, b and r respectively.

y + b = 70
r + b = 80
r + y = 90
(2 × y) + (2 × b) + (2 × r) = 70 + 80 + 90
= 240
y + b + r = 240 ÷ 2 = 120
r = 120 − 70 = 50
y = 120 − 80 = 40
b = 120 − 90 = 30
She has 50 red beads, 40 yellow beads and 30 blue beads.

18. Let the number of blue, yellow and red flags be b, y and r respectively.

b + y = 100
r + b = 90
y + r = 80
(2 × b) + (2 × y) + (2 × r) = 100 + 90 + 80
= 270
y + b + r = 270 ÷ 2 = 135
r = 135 − 100 = 35
y = 135 − 90 = 45
b = 135 − 80 = 55
He sells 35 red flags, 45 yellow flags and 55 blue flags.

Chapter 14 Practice

Page 223

1. excess of pieces of candy = 8
shortage of pieces of candy = 4
Difference of pieces of candy each pupil gets = 10 − 8 = 2
(8 + 4) ÷ 2 = 12 ÷ 2 = 6
The teacher gives the pieces of candy to 6 pupils.
6 × 8 + 8 = 56   or   6 × 10 − 4 = 56
She has 56 pieces of candy.

2. excess of oranges = 3
shortage of oranges = 7
Difference of oranges each family member gets = 7 − 5 = 2
(3 + 7) ÷ 2 = 10 ÷ 2 = 5
There are 5 members in this family.
5 × 5 + 3 = 28   or   5 × 7 − 7 = 28
There are 28 oranges in this carton.

Page 224

3. excess of water = 4 ℓ
shortage of water = 3 ℓ × 4 = 12 ℓ
Difference between the capacity of the two pails = 5 ℓ − 3 ℓ = 2 ℓ
(4 + 12) ÷ 2 = 8
He needs 8 such pails.
8 × 5 ℓ − 4 ℓ = 36 ℓ or
8 × 3 ℓ + 12 ℓ = 36 ℓ
36 ℓ of water are needed to fill the fish tank.

4. excess of students = 5
shortage of students = 40
Difference between the seating capacity of the two buses = 40 − 35 = 5
(5 + 40) ÷ 5 = 45 ÷ 5 = 9
9 buses are needed for the field trip.
9 × 35 + 5 = 320   or
9 × 40 − 40 = 320
320 students are going on the field trip.

978-1-62399-074-9
Singapore Math Challenge

Page 225

5. excess of money = $6
shortage of money = $8
Difference between the cost of a comic and
a mystery book = $5 – $3 = $2
($6 + $8) ÷ $2 = $14 ÷ $2 = 7
Ken is buying 7 comics or mystery books.
7 × $3 + $6 = $27   or
7 × $5 – $8 = $27
He has $27.

6. excess of students = 16
excess of students = 2
Difference of students on each boat
= 5 – 3 = 2
(16 – 2) ÷ 2 = 14 ÷ 2 = 7
There are 7 boats.
7 × 3 + 16 = 37   or
7 × 5 + 2 = 37
 There are 37 students.

Page 226

7. excess of carrots = 7
excess of carrots = 2
Difference of carrots each rabbit would
receive = 4 – 3 = 1
(7 – 2) ÷ 1 = 5
Mrs. Bunny gave the carrots to 5 rabbits.
5 × 3 + 7 = 22   or
5 × 4 + 2 = 22
She had 22 carrots.

Page 227

8. shortage of students = 2 × 6 = 12
excess of students = 3 × 4 = 12
Difference of students in each hostel room
= 6 – 4 = 2
(12 + 12) ÷ 2 = 12
The international school has 12 hostel rooms.
12 × 6 – 12 = 60   or
12 × 4 + 12 = 60
60 students want to stay in the hostel.

Page 228

9. excess of questions to be graded = 5 × 4 = 20
shortage of questions to be graded = 5 × 6
                                                            = 30
Difference between the number of questions
she graded in a minute = 6 – 4 = 2
(20 + 30) ÷ 2 = 25
The time she used for grading was 25 minutes.
25 min. × 4 + 20 = 120   or
25 min. × 6 – 30 = 120
She graded 120 questions before she left the
school.

Page 229

10. shortage = 50 m × 4 = 200
excess = 65 m × 2 = 130
Difference between the two walking speeds
= 65 m/min. – 50 m/min.
= 15 m/min.
(200 m + 130 m) ÷ 15 m/min. = 22
Jodi takes 22 minutes to walk to school in
order to be on time.
22 min. × 50 m + 200 m = 1,300 m   or
22 min. × 65 m – 130 m = 1,300 m
The school is 1,300 m from her house.

Chapter 15 Practice

Page 230

1. **(a)** 1st layer = 3 × 3 = 9
2nd layer = 3 × 2 = 6
3rd layer = 3 × 1 = 3
4th layer = 3 × 1 = 3
Total number of cubes = 9 + 6 + 3 + 3
= 21

 (b) 1st layer = 3 × 2 = 6
2nd layer = 6 – 1 = 5
3rd layer = 3
4th layer = 1
Total number of cubes = 6 + 5 + 3 + 1
= 15

 (c) Each layer = 3 × 3 = 9
Total number of cubes = 9 × 3
= 27

 (d) Total number of cubes = (9 × 3) – 3 – 2
= 22

Page 231

2. **(a)** Total number of cubes
= 9 + 8 + 5 + 5
= 27

 (b) Total number of cubes
= 12 + 9 + 7 + 3
= 31

 (c) Total number of cubes
= 16 + 9 + 4 + 1
= 30

 (d) 1st layer = 3 × 5 = 15 cubes
15 × 3 = 45 cubes
45 – 6 (hollow) = 39 cubes

Page 232

3. **(a)** Total number of cubes = 8 × 4
= 32 cubes

 (b) 1st layer = 4 × 3 = 12
2nd layer = 12 – 2 = 10
3rd layer = 5
4th layer = 3
Total number of cubes = 12 + 10 + 5 + 3
= 30

 (c) Top layer = 3
2nd layer = 5 + 2 = 7
3rd layer = 3 + 2 = 5
1st layer = 7 + 2 = 9
Total number of cubes = 3 + 5 + 7 + 9
= 24

Page 233

4. Visualize the cuboid painted yellow. There will be some cubes not painted yellow at all, and some cubes that are painted yellow on one face, two faces or three faces.

No. of faces painted yellow	0	1	2	3	4	5	6	
No. of cubes	1	6	12	8	0	0	0	Total: 27

Page 234

5.

No. of faces painted blue	0	1	2	3	4	5	6	
No. of cubes	0	0	0	2	3	4	0	Total: 9

Page 235

6.

No. of faces painted green	0	1	2	3	4	5	6	
No. of cubes	0	0	2	2	6	2	0	Total: 12

Chapter 16 Practice

Page 240

1.

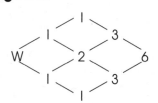

There is only 1 way to form WA and WAT but 2 ways to form WAT for the T at the middle node.

Since (1 + 2) = 3, (2 + 1) = 3, there are 3 ways to form WATE.

Finally, there are (3 + 3) = 6 ways to form the whole word.

Page 241

2. $31 \div 7 = 4 R 3$

This means that 4 days of the week happened 4 times. These were Monday, Tuesday, Wednesday and Thursday.

There were 3 days of the week that happened 5 times: Friday, Saturday and Sunday.

Therefore, January 1st in that year was on Friday.

We may use the table to confirm your answer.

Sun.	Mon.	Tue.	Wed.	Thur.	Fri.	Sat.
31					1	2
3	4	5	6	7	8	9
10	11	12	13	14	15	16
17	18	19	20	21	22	23
24	25	26	27	28	29	30

Page 242

3. Step 1: Divide all the 15 gold coins into 3 groups of 5 coins.

   Step 2: Weigh any 2 such groups.
   The fake coin will be in the lightest among the 3 groups.

   Step 3: Divide the lightest group into 3 groups again. 2 of such groups will have 2 coins.

   Step 4: Weigh the two groups of 2 coins.
   The fake coin is in the lighter group. Otherwise, the remaining coin is the fake coin.

   Step 5: If the fake coin is in the lighter group, weigh each of the coins in that group. The lighter coin is the fake coin.

4. The steps below illustrate how to help Lily get 20 ml of water.

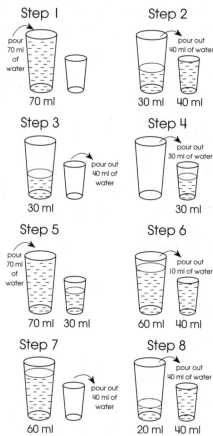

20 ml of water is in the 70-ml cup.

978-1-62399-074-9
Singapore Math Challenge

Page 243

5. Since the area doubled every day, the pond was half-covered with leaves on the 15th day.

6. $31 \div 7 = 4 R 3$
   4 days of the week happened 4 times.
   They were Monday, Tuesday, Wednesday and Thursday.
   3 days of the week happened 5 times.
   They were Friday, Saturday and Sunday.
   The first day in March was on Friday.
   We may use the table below to confirm.

Sun.	Mon.	Tue.	Wed.	Thu.	Fri.	Sat.
31					1	2
3	4	5	6	7	8	9
10	11	12	13	14	15	16
17	18	19	20	21	22	23
24	25	26	27	28	29	30

The 10th of March was on Sunday.

Page 244

7. The ant can travel in 6 ways.

8. This is similar to what you have learned in chapter two.
   $$1 + 2 + 3 + 4 + 5 + 6 + 7 = (8 \times 3) + 4$$
   $$= 28$$
   Each of them would get 1, 2, 3, 4, 5, 6, and 7 carrots respectively.

Page 245

9.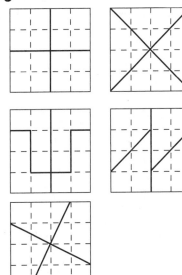

Page 246

10.

One light	Two lights	Three lights	Four lights
Y	YR	YRB	YRBG
R	YB	YRG	
B	YG	YBG	
G	RB	RBG	
	RG		
	BG		

These lights can make 15 different signals.

Page 247

11. Commuters can buy tickets to 5 different train stations:
    $6 \times 5 = 30$
    There are 30 types of train tickets between City A and City B.

978-1-62399-074-9
Singapore Math Challenge

Page 248

12. Let A, B, C, D, E and F be the representation of the 6 people.

A	B	C	D	E	F
5	4	3	2	1	0

$5 + 4 + 3 + 2 + 1 + 0 = 15$

There are 15 handshakes among 6 people.

13.

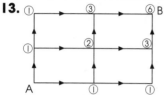

An ant can go from Point A to Point B in 6 ways.

Page 249

14.

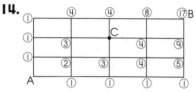

The ant can crawl from Point A to Point B in 17 ways without going through point C.

15. $12 \times 2 = 24$

She could have read 24 pages in these 2 days.

$24 \div 8 = 3$

24 pages were read in 3 days if she finished reading the storybook 2 days in advance.

$12 + 8 = 20$

She read 20 pages a day.

$20 \times 3 = 60$

There were 60 pages in the storybook.

Page 250

16.

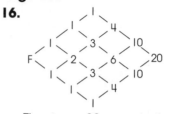

There are 20 ways to form "FLOWERS" as shown in the above network.

Page 251

17. After the 1st round, 2, 4, 6, 8, …, 30 are left.
After the 2nd round, 4, 8, 12, …, 28 are left.
After the 3rd round, 8, 16, 24 are left.
After the last round, the number of the only student in the line was 16.

18. Working backward,

4th minute → Whole surface

3rd minute → $\frac{1}{2}$ of the surface

2nd minute → $\frac{1}{4}$ of the surface

The oil covers $\frac{1}{4}$ of the surface of a bowl of water after 2 minutes.

Page 252

19.

Alice	Beatrice	Cindy	Diana
(5, 8) ✓	(3, 8) ✗	(3, 5) ✗	(1, 3)
(6, 7) ✗	(4, 7) ✓	(2, 6) ✓	
		(5, 6) ✗	(1, 7) ✗

Diana will draw two cards numbered 1 and 3 respectively.

20. 14th day → 40 mm
13th day → 20 mm
12th day → 10 mm
11th day → 5 mm
It took 11 days to grow to 5 mm.

978-1-62399-074-9
Singapore Math Challenge

Chapter 17 Practice

Page 257

1. The smallest divisor is 7.

   $\boxed{} \div 7 = 8\,R\,6$

   By working backward,

   $7 \times 8 + 6 = 62$

   $\boxed{62} \div \boxed{7} = 8\,R\,6$

2. The largest remainder is 5.

   $\boxed{} \div 6 = 8\,R\,5$

   By working backward,

   $6 \times 8 + 5 = 53$

   $\boxed{53} \div 6 = 8\,R\,\boxed{5}$

Page 258

3. $37 \div \boxed{10} = \boxed{3}\,R\,7$

4. $\square \div 6 = 5\,R\,5$　$6 \times 5 + 5 = 35$

   $\square \div 6 = 4\,R\,4$　$6 \times 4 + 4 = 28$

   $\square \div 6 = 3\,R\,3$　$6 \times 3 + 3 = 21$

   $\square \div 6 = 2\,R\,2$　$6 \times 2 + 2 = 14$

   $\square \div 6 = 1\,R\,1$　$6 \times 1 + 1 = 7$

   The possible dividends are 7, 14, 21, 28 and 35.

Page 259

5. $24 \div 5 = 4\,R\,4$

●	●	●	○	○
R1	R2	R3	R4	0

   The color of the 24th bead is white.

   $198 \div 5 = 39\,R\,3$

   The 198th bead is black.

6. The pattern repeats after every 6 shapes.

   $38 \div 6 = 6\,R\,2$

○	○	△	△	△	□
R1	R2	R3	R4	R5	0

   The shape of the 38th figure is a ○.

   $59 \div 6 = 9\,R\,5$

   The shape of the 59th figure is a △.

Page 260

7. $28 \div 3 = 9\,R\,1$

3	2	4
R1	R2	0

   The digit of the 28th number is 3.

   $3 + 2 + 4 = 9$

   $33 \div 3 = 11$ blocks of 9

   $11 \times 9 = 99$

   The sum of the first 33 numbers is 99.

8. $35 \div 4 = 8\,R\,3$

3	6	4	5
R1	R2	R3	0

   The 35th number is 4.

   $3 + 6 + 4 + 5 = 18$

   $18 \div 4 = 4$ blocks of 18 + the first 2 numbers

   $(4 \times 18) + 3 + 6 = 72 + 9 = 81$

   The sum of the first 18 numbers is 81.

Page 261

9. $25 \div 7 = 3\,R\,4$

Sun.	Mon.	Tue.	Wed.	Thurs.	Fri.	Sat.
0	R1	R2	R3	R4	R5	R6

   July 25th in that year was on Thursday.

10. $31 - 10 = 21$

    $21 + 1 = 22$

    There are 22 days from March 10th to March 31st.

    There are 30 days in the month of April.

    $22 + 30 + 11 = 63$ days

    There are 63 days from March 10th to May 11th.

    $63 \div 7 = 9$

Sun.	Mon.	Tue.	Wed.	Thurs.	Fri.	Sat.
R6	0	R1	R2	R3	R4	R5

    May 11th in that year was on Monday.

Page 262

11. | Jessica | Melissa | Natalie | Alison | Kelly |
    |---------|---------|---------|--------|-------|
    | R1 | R2 | R3 | R4 | 0 |

    $48 \div 5 = 9\,R\,3$

    Natalie will get the last card.

12. | Carson | Joan | Chloe | Amanda |
    |--------|------|-------|--------|
    | R1 | R2 | R3 | R4 |
    | 0 | R7 | R6 | R5 |

    $36 \div 8 = 4\,R\,4$

    Amanda will get the last card.

978-1-62399-074-9
Singapore Math Challenge

Page 263

13.

Sun.	Mon.	Tue.	Wed.	Thurs.	Fri.	Sat.
R2	R3	R4	R5	R6	0	R1

$10 + 30 = 40$

$40 \div 7 = 5 R 5$

It would be a Wednesday 30 days later.

14.

A	B	C	D	E	F
R1	R2	R3	R4	R5	0

$150 \div 6 = 25$

Florence will get the 150th card.

$200 \div 6 = 33 R 2$

Ben will get the last card.

Page 264

15. $149 - 5 = 144$

$144 \div 12 = 12$ $144 \div 16 = 9$

$144 \div 18 = 8$ $144 \div 24 = 6$

$144 \div 36 = 4$ $144 \div 72 = 2$

All the 2-digit divisors are 12, 16, 18, 24, 36 and 72.

16. Multiples of 3:

   3, 6, 9, 12, 15, 18, 21, 24, …

   + 2: 5, 8, ⑪, 14, 17, 20, ㉓, 26, …

   Multiples of 4:

   4, 8, 12, 16, 20, 24, 28, 32, …

   + 3: 7, ⑪, 15, 19, ㉓, 27, 31, 35, …

   Two such numbers that are smaller than 30 are 11 and 23.

Page 265

17. It is easier to start with the multiples of bigger numbers.

   Multiples of 7:

   7, 14, 21, 28, 35, …

   + 2: 9, 16, ㉓, 30, 37, …

   Multiples of 5:

   5, 10, 15, 20, 25, 30, …

   + 3: 8, 13, 18, ㉓, 28, 33, …

   The number is 23.

18. □ ÷ □ = 9 R 2

   Use guess-and-check method,

   $39 \div 3 = 13 R 0$

   $38 \div 4 = 9 R 2$

   38 (dividend) + 4 (divisor) = 42

   The dividend is 38 and the divisor is 4.

Page 266

19. □ ÷ □ = 5 R 6

   Use guess-and-check method,

   $50 \div 12 = 4 R 2$

   $48 \div 10 = 4 R 8$

   $46 \div 8 = 5 R 6$

   46 (dividend) – 8 (divisor) = 38

   The dividend is 46 and the divisor is 8.

20. $90 \times 4 = 360$

   $80 \times 5 = 400$

   The book must be more than 360 pages but less than 400 pages.

   number of pages she reads every day = number of days she takes to finish reading

   $18 \times 18 = 324$

   This is not in the range of 360 to 400 pages.

   $19 \times 19 = 361$

   She must read 19 pages every day.

Chapter 18 Practice

Page 270

1. **(a)** 2 + 2 + 2 + 2 = 8 cm

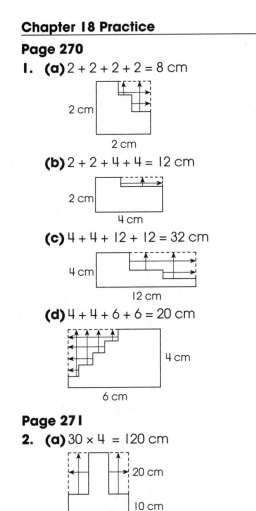

(b) 2 + 2 + 4 + 4 = 12 cm

(c) 4 + 4 + 12 + 12 = 32 cm

(d) 4 + 4 + 6 + 6 = 20 cm

Page 271

2. **(a)** 30 × 4 = 120 cm

(b) 5 × 2 + 6 × 2 = 10 + 12
= 22 cm
22 + 1 + 1 = 24 cm

(c) 9 × 2 + 10 × 2 = 18 + 20
= 38 cm
38 + 2 + 2 = 42 cm

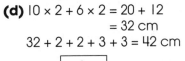

(d) 10 × 2 + 6 × 2 = 20 + 12
= 32 cm
32 + 2 + 2 + 3 + 3 = 42 cm

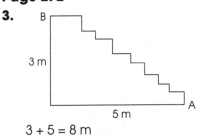

Page 272

3.

3 + 5 = 8 m

4. The figure has 12 sides altogether.
36 ÷ 12 = 3
The length of each side of a square is 3 cm.

Page 273

5. After dividing, each rectangle becomes like what is shown below.

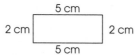

2 + 2 + 5 + 5 = 14
The perimeter of each small rectangle is 14 cm.

6. The figure has 16 sides altogether.
16 × 6 = 96
Its perimeter is 96 cm.

Page 274

7. 8 × 4 = 32
The perimeter of the square is 32 cm.
84 − 32 = 52
The perimeter of the rectangle is 52 cm.
10 × 2 = 20
52 − 20 = 32
32 ÷ 2 = 16
The length of the rectangle is 16 cm.

8. 28 ÷ 4 = 7
Each side of square A is 7 cm.
7 − 2 = 5
Each side of square B is 5 cm.
7 × 3 + 5 × 3 = 21 + 15
= 36
36 + 2 = 38
The perimeter of the figure is 38 cm.

Page 275

9. 15 × 4 = 60
The perimeter of the square is 60 cm.
150 − 60 = 90
The perimeter of the rectangle is 90 cm.
25 × 2 = 50
90 − 50 = 40
40 ÷ 2 = 20
Its width is 20 cm.

10.

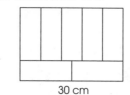

30 ÷ 5 = 6
The width of each rectangle is 6 cm.
15 + 6 = 21
The width of the figure is 21 cm.
21 + 21 + 30 + 30 = 102
The perimeter of the figure is 102 cm.

Page 276

11. 15 × 4 = 60
The perimeter of the square is 60 cm.
60 × 2 = 120
The perimeter of the rectangle is 120 cm.
15 × 2 = 30
120 − 30 = 90
90 ÷ 2 = 45
The length of the rectangle is 45 cm.

12.

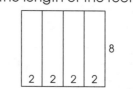

Since the sides of the square are equal, we figure out the length of the rectangle is 8 cm.
2 + 2 + 8 + 8 = 20
The perimeter of each rectangle is 20 cm.
8 × 4 = 32
The perimeter of the square is 32 cm.

Page 277

13. Figure A has 10 equal sides while Figure B has 20 equal sides.

$25 \times 2 = 50$

The perimeter of Figure B is 50 cm.

14. $14 \times 4 = 56$

The perimeter of the square is 56 cm.

$56 \div 8 = 7$ cm

$7 \times 3 = 21$ cm

The length and width of the rectangle are 21 cm and 7 cm respectively.

Chapter 19 Practice

Page 283

1. Page 1 to Page 9: 9 digits

Page 10 to Page 99: 180 digits

Page 100 to Page 185: $185 - 100 = 85$

$85 + 1 = 86$ page numbers

$86 \times 3 = 258$ digits

$9 + 180 + 258 = 447$

447 digits are used for printing the page numbers of the book.

2. Number 1 to 9: 9 digits

Number 10 to Number 99: 180 digits

Number 100 to Number 200: $200 - 100 = 100$

$100 + 1 = 101$ numbers

$101 \times 3 = 303$ digits

$9 + 180 + 303 = 492$

There are 492 digits from numbers 1 to 200.

Page 284

3. Page 1 to Page 9: 9 digits

Page 10 to Page 99: 180 digits

Page 100 to Page 345: $345 - 100 = 245$

$245 + 1 = 246$ page numbers

$246 \times 3 = 738$ digits

$9 + 180 + 738 = 927$

927 digits are in a book that has 345 pages.

4. Number 1 to Number 9: 9 digits

Number to 10 to Number 99: 180 digits

Number 100 to Number 500: $500 - 100 = 400$

$400 + 1 = 401$ numbers

$401 \times 3 = 1,203$ digits

$9 + 180 + 1,203 = 1,392$

There are 1,392 digits from numbers 1 to 500.

978-1-62399-074-9
Singapore Math Challenge

Page 285

5. Page 1 to Page 9: 9 digits
Page 10 to Page 99: 180 digits
648 – 9 – 180 = 459
459 is a 3-digit number.
459 ÷ 3 = 153 pages
99 + 153 = 252
The book has 252 pages.

6. 792 – 9 – 180 = 603 digits
603 ÷ 3 = 201 pages
99 + 201 = 300
The book has 300 pages.

Page 286

7. 1,014 – 9 – 180 = 825 digits
825 ÷ 3 = 275 pages
99 + 275 = 374
The book has 374 pages.

8. 1,248 – 9 – 180 = 1,059 digits
1,059 ÷ 3 = 353 pages
99 + 353 = 452
The book has 452 pages.

Chapter 20 Practice

Page 290

1. **(a)** Formed by 1 Δ = 3
Formed by 2 Δs = 2
Formed by 3 Δs = 1
Total: 3 + 2 + 1 = 6
(b) Formed by 1 Δ = 4
Formed by 2 Δs = 3
Formed by 3 Δs = 2
Formed by 4 Δs = 1
Total: 4 + 3 + 2 + 1 = 10

2. **(a)** Formed by 1 □ = 6
Formed by 4 □s = 2
Total: 6 + 2 = 8
(b) Formed by 1 □ = 9
Formed by 4 □s = 2
Total: 9 + 2 = 11

Page 291

3. **(a)** Formed by 1 Δ = 3
Formed by 2 Δs = 2
Formed by 1 Δ, 1 ◇ = 2
Formed by all = 1
Total = 3 + 2 + 2 + 1
= 8
(b) Formed by 1 Δ = 5
Formed by 2 Δs = 4
Formed by 3 Δs = 2
Formed by 5 Δs = 1
Total = 5 + 4 + 2 + 1
= 12

4. **(a)** 1 □ = 4
2 □s = 4
4 □s = 1
Total = 4 + 4 + 1
= 9
(b) 1 □ = 9
2 □s = 12
3 □s = 6
4 □s = 4
6 □s = 4
9 □s = 1
Total = 9 + 12 + 6 + 4 + 4 + 1
= 36

Page 292

5. **(a)** Formed by 1 Δ = 8
Formed by 2 Δs = 5
Formed by 3 Δs = 6
Formed by 4 Δs = 2
Formed by 5 Δs = 2
Formed by 8 Δs = 1
Total: 8 + 5 + 6 + 2 + 2 + 1 = 24

   (b) Formed by 1 Δ = 3
Formed by 2 Δs = 2
Formed by 1 Δ 1 △ = 2
Formed by 3 Δs 1 △ = 1
Total: 3 + 2 + 2 + 1 = 8

6. Formed by 1 □ = 12
Formed by 2 □s = 16
Formed by 3 □s = 8
Formed by 4 □s = 9
Formed by 6 □s = 4
Formed by 8 □s = 2
Total: 12 + 16 + 8 + 9 + 4 + 2 = 51

Page 293

7. **(a)** Formed by 1 Δ = 10
Formed by 2 Δs = 10
Formed by 3 Δs = 5
Formed by 4 Δs 1 ⬠ = 5
Formed by 2 Δs 1 ⬠ = 5
Total: 10 + 10 + 5 + 5 + 5 = 35

   (b) Formed by 1 Δ = 8
Formed by 2 Δs = 8
Formed by 3 Δs = 4
Formed by 4 Δs = 4
Total: 8 + 8 + 4 + 4 = 24